# Flexibility under Islamic Law

L. Ali Khan

Founder, Legal Scholar Academy and Professor of Law Washburn University

"God desires every convenience for you; He does not want to put you to
hardship."

QUR'AN, *sura al-Baqara* 2:185.

# Table of Contents

# Preface

This booklet has been in writing for several years. It was originally written as a law review article. However, that was not meant to be. The decision to publish it as a small book will hopefully expand its availability in the Muslim world and elsewhere. Islamic law founded on mercy does not wish to punish violations but to make amends for both the wrongdoers and victims. Any spiteful enforcement of the letter of the law is contrary to Islamic ethos based on forgiveness. Islamic law proposes inverse connectivity between flexibility and hardship: Flexibility mitigates hardship while rigidity aggravates hardship. In Islamic law, flexibility is the organizing norm of legal intelligence in its manifestations. Generally, hardship restricts personal freedom and impedes human happiness, social harmony, and economic prosperity. In contrast, many benefits radiate from flexibility. Flexibility facilitates the performance of obligations, bending without abandoning the concepts of time, and place commitments. Flexibility serves as an accommodation principle for persons with disabilities. By removing hardship, flexibility supports convenience and creativity. Creative minds and creative enterprises seldom thrive in rigid structures; they need fluid and flexible settings. Finally, flexibility endorses a concept of adaptable normativity under which each generation of jurists is free to interpret the founding sources of Islamic law, the Qur'an and Prophet's Sunnah. This book urges legal systems, Muslims and non-Muslims, to incorporate flexibility as the supreme principle of legal intelligence manifested in legislation, adjudication, and law enforcement.

Topeka, Kansas, 2019.

# Introduction

In exploring the connectivity between flexibility and hardship, this book contests the popular caricatures of Islam as a religion of uncompromising fanaticism. State-sponsored punishments such as beheadings and the rise of violence associated with militant movements across the world present Islamic law as harsh in content and rigid in the application. The jurisprudential story of Islamic law, however, is much different from its current versions practiced in militant circles and some Muslim national systems. At the core of the story are the unified concepts of convenience and flexibility that mitigate individual and communitarian hardships.

Flexibility is a prescriptive principle of leniency, forgiveness, and mercy in enforcing Islamic law in various contexts. Functionally, flexibility removes hardship, rigidity, ruthlessness, and cruelty from the realm of law and legal reasoning. The flexibility principle is not a juristic concoction inducted into Islamic law. It is a divine principle that emanates from the Qur'an and the Prophet's Sunnah, the two primary sources of Islamic law, which constitute the Basic Code of Islam.[1] The Qur'an reveals the flexibility principle through the notion of *yus'r*,[2] an Arabic word, which means convenience, ease, relief, or facility. Ontologically, the flexibility principle presupposes that the human world is dynamic, amorphous, and imperfect. Social phenomenology needs order and regulation but it can avoid strict categories. An overly-

3

conceptual, perfectionist or mechanistic conception of law fails to capture the elasticity of human life, causing more harm than benefit. Flexibility, as explained below, is a valuable contribution to the world's legal systems, including common law that has benefitted from various concepts of Islamic law.[3] In the past two hundred years, the trend of borrowing has shifted. Muslim states now extensively acquire substantive law, codes of procedures, and legal methods from civil law and common law traditions.[4] In receiving the law from Western legal systems, Muslim lawmakers, jurists, and judges must not overlook the flexibility principle.

Relying on the notion of *yus'r*, the Basic Code highlights the natural connectivity between flexibility and convenience. Flexibility safeguards convenience, and convenience seeks flexibility. For example, God says that He has revealed the Qur'an as an easy scripture for the convenience of readers.[5] This convenience preserves the Qur'an as a universal holy book for diverse populations with differing histories, cultures, and languages. In this sense, the Qur'an is meta-lingual and not confined to the Arabic text.[6] In mitigating the difficulty of fasting for someone who is ill or traveling, the Qur'an states: "God desires every convenience for you; He does not want to put you to hardship."[7] Likewise, God offsets His commands with convenience to reward believers: "But as for one who believes and does righteousness, he will have a reward of Paradise, and we will speak to him from our command with convenience."[8] Comforting human beings facing adversity, the Qur'an affirms: "Verily, with every difficulty, there is a relief."[9] The flexibility principle, which constitutes the essence of Islamic law, alleviates hardships and offers conveniences in solving problems,[10] allowing obligors to fulfill their religious and legal duties without suffering severe spatiotemporal constrictions and other difficulties.

The Prophet's Sunnah, the second primary source of Islamic law, reinforces the flexibility principle. Whenever the Prophet ordered his followers to do something, he assigned them tasks easy for them to do and not tasks beyond their strength or endurance.[11] This principle of convenience was extended even to relations with non-Muslims.[12] The Prophet said, "Make things easy for the people, and do not make it difficult for them, and make them calm (with glad tidings) and do not repulse (them)." Thoughtless enforcement of prescribed behaviors is offensive to Islamic legal intelligence.[13]

Significant harm is inflicted on communities when any codes of behavior are mechanistically applied, disregarding varying circumstances and consequences.[14] A sophisticated normative enterprise is highly flexible as it is sensitive to variation in facts and contexts. In the United States, for example, the equal protection of law may consider phenomenal differences and circumstantial distinctiveness.[15] The law "does not require things which are different in fact or opinion to be treated in law as though they were the same."[16]

Rejecting the mechanical notion of equality, the Basic Code treats individuals as unique human beings with varying capacities to undertake difficulty. Some individuals are physically strong and endure more massive assignments; some are frail; some are emotionally sturdy and tolerate extensive adversity; some are fragile. Islamic law does not blindly burden all persons with the same duties ignoring individual capacities. "On no soul does God place a burden greater than it can bear."[17]The flexibility principle guides Islamic law in accommodating individual differences and varying circumstances.[18]

Jurisprudentially, flexibility occupies an intermediate space between arbitrariness and rigidity. Arbitrariness occurs when there exist no rules, when rules are abruptly altered without notice, or when it is uncertain whether the rules would be enforced.[19] Selective enforcement of rules based on prejudice or preference is symptomatic of arbitrariness, though inadequate resources may compel partial enforcement of rules.[20] Rigidity is the opposite of arbitrariness.

Rigidity occurs when rules are applied even though the outcome is unjust or even shocking.[21]Rigidity also occurs when narrow rules carry no exceptions, when rules disregard complex facts, or when rules impose avoidable hardships.[22] Mediating between arbitrariness and rigidity, the flexibility principle demands that rules be made and enforced. However, flexibility may bend the rules to accommodate complex facts, avoid unjust outcomes, and provide relief in cases of hardship. Islamic flexibility requires a sophisticated understanding of rules. If applied without prudence, flexibility may slide into arbitrariness.

It might be argued that flexibility risks undermining the rule of law as it authorizes legal officials to bend the rules to achieve what they think is fair and just. This argument is valid, as explained above if flexibility turns into arbitrariness. The purpose of flexibility, however, is to fuse convenience in every aspect of life and minimize the unnecessary difficulty in meeting legal and contractual obligations. In easing the difficulty, flexibility does not diminish rights and obligations emanating from legal relations. Nor does flexibility undermine scheduling or observing punctuality in future meetings, events, departures, and arrivals.

Respect for spatiotemporal commitments is an indispensable part of the law, and no concept of flexibility can be allowed to disrupt mutual expectations tied to time and place.[23] Understood correctly, the flexibility principle is the backbone of the rule of law. It does not compromise core commitments even though it might not fully enforce the peripherals in all cases. With its primary focus on the core and not the circumference, flexibility protects social, economic, and legal relations; it improves efficiency, productivity, working conditions, and personal satisfaction.

Flexibility is compatible with the modern notion of flextime, a notion designed to distinguish between core and peripheral commitments. Narrowly defined, flextime means that employees may schedule their work hours, disregarding the peripheral nine-to-five workday.[24] Parents with small children may work more compressed or dispersed hours to meet work and family obligations. The flexibility principle includes the concept of flex-place, allowing the freedom to work from places other than offices.[25] For example, employees may work from homes, cafes, parks, and other places, depending on the nature of work. [26]However, workplace constraints cannot be abandoned in certain types of work. Building roads and bridges, for example, would require that workers arrive at the place where the bridge is being built. Even if the workplace is indispensable, flexibility may creatively design a system under which the workers can choose the hours they are at the workplace.[27] Thus, the flexibility principle is much more extensive in granting conveniences than allowing employees to personalize the workday.

Flexibility recognizes a common observation: Everything changes in the phenomenal world. At its core, therefore, the flexibility principle cherishes fluidity, variety, diversity, plurality, vicissitudes, variations, vagaries, differences, and other dimensions of change. Stringency and uniformity, though useful in some contexts, may not be compatible with the theory and practice of flexibility. If the workday is nonflexible, employees lose options to adjust personal schedules. If a rule is rigid, it does not accommodate variations. If an institution seeks uniformity, it will not tolerate diversity.

If a single path is laid out to reach the goal, reaching the goal through alternative paths is considered deviant. The flexibility principle is an innovative way of thinking; it is a productive mindset; it is a resourceful organizing principle; it is inspired consciousness; it is imaginative accommodation of individual predicaments and social relations. Because of its intrinsic tractability, the flexibility principle challenges mechanistic structures of thought processes. As this book explains, the flexibility principle shapes normative cognition.

Analytically, the book is structured in the following sequence. Chapter 1 explains legal minimalism as a founding principle of Islamic law. Chapter 2 explains Islamic temporality, explaining how Islam demystifies time and presents it as a standard to measure durations. Chapter 3 explains how Islamic law allows flexibility in meeting legal, contractual, and spiritual obligations. Part IV demonstrates that the flexibility principle recognizes personal differences that may be ignored in over-commitment to equality and standardization. Chapter 4 discusses the Islamic understanding of dreams and their role in creativity and future visions. Chapter 5 examines creativity as a form of flexibility. Chapter 6 presents adaptable normativity in that each generation of Muslims has a right to receive God's Law in its wisdom. Finally, the book concludes that contemporary Muslim communities will significantly benefit if they incorporate the flexibility principle in social, spiritual, legal, creative, and interpretive domains. Non-Islamic legal systems may similarly benefit from the flexibility principle.

# Chapter 1

## Legal Minimalism

Legal minimalism, a founding principle of Islamic law, requires that there be fewest rules to regulate social and economic life.[28] Legal minimalism assures flexibility in social and legal relations as people, in the absence of regulations, can freely choose what is good for them. When the law is overly regulatory, it superimposes a coercive framework over an otherwise amorphous phenomenology of human life. Legal minimalism protects the freedom of human behavior by renouncing the boot-camping of social order. It deters governments from encroaching upon personal freedoms and private decision-making. In some regimes, particularly under authoritarian and unjust governments, overregulation emanates from desires to control rather than from practical knowledge and wisdom. In some systems, including well-functioning democracies, overregulation is a form of benevolent state paternalism founded on the premise that the people lack the intelligence, information, or will to make judicious decisions. Islamic legal minimalism rejects both authoritarian and benevolent state paternalism.

Embracing minimalism as a paradigmatic principle of law, the Qur'an instructs believers not to demand too many rules: "O you who believe, do not ask about things which, if they are shown to you, will distress you."[29] This verse was revealed to deter a deeply-entrenched local habit of the people of Medina, including believers and non-believers, who asked the Prophet too many questions.[30] Some asked questions to make fun of the Prophet.[31] Some asked questions to test the Prophet's knowledge. Some asked questions to make sure that their conduct did not breach any part of divine law.[32] Regardless of the questioner's motive, the Prophet discouraged Muslims from demanding too many rigid and precise rules. The Prophet's unshakeable trust in legal minimalism was most evident when Muslims, after the conquest of Makkah, were performing the hajj and asking a series of questions about the rituals. The Prophet relied on the flexibility principle to answer all these questions.[33]

In Islam, legal minimalism is enforced through several distinct methodologies. Two are noteworthy. First, Islamic legal minimalism rejects the idea that rules ought to be absolute. On the contrary, Islamic law found in the Basic Code is diluted with exceptions and exemptions. Legal minimalism is incompatible with the jurisprudence of rigid or simplistic rules that apply under all conditions and circumstances. Flexible rules that absorb a variety of facts are more consistent with legal minimalism than linear rules constructed and enforced without conditions and exceptions. Second, narrowing the scope of a rule is consistent with legal minimalism as is refusing to expand a rule's application. Legal minimalism is defeated when a rule is interpreted to expand its coverage, substantive scope, or territorial reach. The Basic Code rarely permits the expansion of a punitive rule to cast a wider net. It, however, allows the contraction of a rule's coverage, substantive scope, and territorial reach.

To understand practical applications of legal minimalism, consider the case of unlawful sexuality under the Basic Code. Legal minimalism includes minimal enforcement of prescribed punishments. As a general principle, the Qur'an prohibits and punishes non-marital sexuality. "And do not approach unlawful sexual intercourse (*zina*). Indeed, it is ever an immorality and is evil as a way."[34] This explicit prohibition guides Muslims not to engage in any form of non-marital sexuality, called *zina*, including pre-marital and extra-marital sexuality. The Qur'an prescribes a punishment of one hundred lashes for men and women who commit *zina*.[35] However, this punishment is reserved for persons not married at the time of committing *zina*. The Prophet's Sunnah prescribes the punishment of stoning to death if a married person commits *zina*.[36]

Despite stiff punishments, the law against *zina* offers a perfect example of legal minimalism. Several motes have been built around the offense of *zina* so that the prescribed punishments are rarely carried out. The Prophet narrowed the definition of *zina* in a case brought before him. When a person came to the Prophet to confess the offense of *zina*, the Prophet made sure that the person understood what *zina* meant, thus setting a precedent that even the subject matter of a confession needs to be verified. The Prophet made clear to the person that kissing, winking, or mere looking (with lustful eyes) does not constitute *zina*. [37] The Prophet restricted the offense of *zina* to strictly genital intercourse.[38]This definitional restriction for the purpose of punishment was needed since the concept of *zina* in the broad sense included the *zina* of eyes, *zina* of the heart, *zina* of mere physical touch, and the like.[39]

In yet another case of legal minimalism, the Prophet showed reluctance to even hearing a confession of *zina*.[40] A person came to the Prophet and confessed *zina*. The Prophet turned his face away from the confessor. The person walked to the other side and confessed again. The Prophet turned his face away from the confessor.[41] These gestures suggested to the audience that confession of the offense of *zina* is not obligatory. The offender may seek God's forgiveness and not subject himself or herself to the prescribed punishment, particularly if the person is married and would be stoned to death. The Basic Code discourages the confession of *zina*.

In order to subject the offense of *zina* to further legal minimalism, the Basic Code requires a strong proof. "And those who accuse chaste women and then do not produce four witnesses - lash them with eighty lashes and do not accept from them testimony ever after. And those are defiantly disobedient."[42] Rarely would someone engage in any form of sexuality, let alone unlawful sexuality, in the presence of four witnesses? This high proof, therefore, is designed to deter non-marital sexuality without making it easy for the legal system to punish *zina*. Even if four witnesses are available, the Qur'an allows the offender to repent and reform, in which case the punishment of *zina* is not inflicted.[43] With all these conditions and concessions, the Basic Code subjects the enforcement of *zina* to legal minimalism.[44]

The Basic Code adopts the principle of non-retroactivity to exclude the application of laws to past behaviors. This principle is a form of legal minimalism. Retroactivity is the expansion of a rule backward in time. As a matter of universal jurisprudence in modern legal systems, most rules are prospective and regulate behavior engaged in after the enactment of a rule. For example, the U.S. Constitution prohibits the passing of ex post facto law, a clear deviation from the common law tradition that had allowed retroactivity.[45] Forerunning jurisprudential modernity by nearly fourteen centuries, the Basic Code does not permit the *ex post facto* application of a rule to cases that occurred before the enactment of the rule. For example, the Qur'an strictly prohibits the charging of interest on loans. However, the prohibition was not applied to interest-bearing loans made before the pronouncement of the rule. "So whoever has received an admonition from his Lord and desists may have (keep the interest) what is past, and his affair rests with

15

Allah."[46]Thus, non-retroactivity preserves legal minimalism as it excludes past behaviors from the reach of a new rule.

Legal minimalism also requires that some rules be suspended under exceptional circumstances. Of course, some rules, such as the right against torture, are immune from suspension. In most legal systems, rules without circumstantial exceptions are rare.[47] Each rule presupposes a set of circumstances, a factual context. For example, speed limits (maximum and minimum) on a highway presuppose fair weather. Speed limits are inapplicable if the highway is overly-crowded or visibility is exceptionally low. Under adverse road conditions, most motorists know that they cannot drive at the prescribed speed limits. They adjust for speed, even going below the prescribed minimal speed, to assure safety. Rules that must be enforced regardless of facts are inherently flawed. Accordingly, most rules are fact-sensitive in that rules are bent and even suspended to resolve issues arising under exceptional circumstances.

The rules of behavior found in the Basic Code are seldom absolute, to be enforced under all circumstances. The Basic Code relaxes the rules to accommodate exceptional circumstances and acts of mercy.[48] As explained below, Islamic normativity is blended with circumstantial exceptions derived from necessity and generosity derived from mercy. Both necessity and mercy are the fountains of flexibility. They both summon the suspension of rules in specific cases. Necessity highlights exceptional circumstances of

16

hard cases, whereas mercy highlights the munificence of the victim or the victim's family in pardoning wrongdoers in specific cases.

## A. Necessity as a Source of Flexibility

The Basic Code lays out right and wrong, lawful (halal) and unlawful (haram), providing a code of behavior. For example, it is unlawful for believers to consume pork. However, this prohibition is relaxed under the dictates of necessity. As explained below, if there is nothing else to eat, eating pork is permissible for survival. Thus the rule prohibiting eating pork is not rigidly enforced under all circumstances.

The following verse of the Quran lays out the parameters of what might be called necessity-flexibility: "He (God) has only forbidden you carrion, blood, and swine, and that which has been consecrated to any other than God. But who is driven by necessity, neither craving nor transgressing, it is no sin for him. For God is Forgiving, Compassionate."[49] A plain reading of the verse clarifies that God relaxes the prohibitory rules because divine normativity is interfused with forgiveness and compassion. A person eating pork for survival is forgiven and not punished for violating the rule. This forgiveness demonstrates that the enforcement of divine rules cannot be detached from divine compassion.

This commandment distinguishes between genuine necessity and manufactured necessity. An intense craving for eating a prohibited item, when halal food is available, cannot constitute genuine necessity. Taste preferences or gastronomic cravings for prohibited items are ruled out of the realm of genuine necessity. Similarly, genuine necessity is more than mere objective factum; it has an important element of intention. A person suffering from genuine necessity has no pre-necessity longing for violating the rule. If a person is looking for an opportunity to violate a rule, the person may manufacture a necessity to justify deviation from the rule. Note that the necessity-flexibility is not confined to food. Food examples furnish a convenient way to understand other applications of necessity-based flexibility.

To further expand the realm of flexibility, the Quran clarifies that what is not forbidden is permissible: "And why do you not eat of that [meat] over which the name of God has been mentioned, when He has explained to you that which is forbidden to you, unless you are compelled by necessity. But many mislead [others] by their own desires without knowledge. Your Lord knows best those who transgress."[50] This commandment discourages rulers and jurists from reducing the realm of permissibility by adding prohibitions.

## B. Mercy as a Source of Flexibility

In addition to necessity, mercy, as a source of flexibility, also enlightens Islamic law. Just like a necessity, mercy may be invoked to suspend or abandon the application of a rule. The notion of mercy may be employed to forgive a loan that the debtor

18

cannot pay.  Mercy may be invoked to forgive tortfeasance and personal wrongs, including physical, monetary, and reputational injuries. Mercy is most meaningful in pardoning crimes and suspending fines and punishments. The exercise of mercy has few limits. It may be wielded in pardoning petty misdemeanors. As discussed below, however, mercy may be exercised in serious crimes, such as murder.

The Qur'an classifies the murder as *qisas*, an Arabic word, which means retribution.[51] Not all crimes under Islamic law are classified as *qisas*.[52] In addition to murder, Muslim states have expanded the law of *qisas* to include other bodily injuries.[53] Laying out the law of *qisas*, the Qur'an states:

> "O you who believe! Al-qisas is prescribed for you in case of murder: the free for the free, the slave for the slave, and the female for the female. But if the killer is forgiven by the brother (or the relatives, etc.) of the killed against blood money, then adhering to it with fairness and payment of the blood money, to the heir should be made in fairness. This is an alleviation and a mercy from your Lord. So after this whoever transgresses the limits (i.e. kills the killer after taking the blood money), he shall have a painful torment."[54]

This commandment grants three options to the victim's family of the murdered. The victim's family may demand the execution of the murderer. The victim's family may settle for blood money or the victim's family may forgive the murderer. Note that the verse invokes the notion of God's mercy in expanding remedies within the realm of *qisas*. The Qur'an recognizes life for a life as a retaliatory remedy but not the only remedy. The Qur'an weakens the pre-Islamic canon of revenge by providing a powerful material incentive to accept blood money and a powerful spiritual incentive to pardon the murderer without any blood money.

In 2011, Amanah Bahrami, an Iranian woman, pardoned the man who threw acid on her face causing severe disfigurement. First, the victim demanded *qisas* and settled for a judicial punishment that would have blinded the perpetrator, a punishment heavily criticized in the human rights circles. On the day when the punishment of *qisas* was scheduled to be enforced, however, Brahami pardoned the perpetrator without demanding any blood money.[55]

Contrary to the popular views of Islam in non-Muslim communities, which highlight Muslims' hard-heartedness, mercy is deeply suffused in Islamic consciousness. This is so because God is merciful, a revelation repeated numerous times in the Qur'an.[56] As explained below, there is one law that God has prescribed for himself, and that is to be merciful.[57] Though God does justice, God's mercy dominates everything God does. Because God is merciful, Muslims cannot be otherwise. God's mercy is an invitation to all believers to be merciful.

Cruelty is the opposite of mercy and cannot be any part of Islamic law. If mercy dilutes the sting of law, cruelty adds poison to it. In enforcing Islamic law, state officials, as well as private litigants, must not deviate from the dictates of mercy and resort to cruelty. Under no circumstances can jurists and judges add cruelty to the interpretations of the law. For example, the Islamic flexibility principle does not allow the inclusion of torture as an enforcement instrument for purposes of national security. After the 9/11 terrorist attacks, the United States officials, including lawyers, argued for the employment of unprecedented harsh investigative techniques to obtain information from Muslim militants detained at Guantanamo prison. Their arguments, though defended under the laws of the United States, will muster no legitimacy under Islamic law. Even though some Muslim states are notorious for resorting to torture in dealing with what they also call "terrorists," they cannot invoke any principle of Islamic law to support their policy of cruelty. The cruelty perpetrated in a Muslim state has no normative basis in Islamic law as it violates the principle of mercy that cannot be suspended under any circumstances.

In all matters of creation, God's justice is suffused with a generous margin of mercy. In fact, according to the Qur'an, the margin of mercy is a law that God has prescribed for Himself.[58] God exercises mandatory mercy to judge personal digressions, violations of laws, and acts of disobedience. Even when His wrath is inevitable, God does not abandon the margin of mercy. God's mercy is accommodative. His margin of mercy applies to all violations and infractions, whether the perpetrator is depraved, recidivist, or incorrigible.

Furthermore, the margin of mercy applies to individuals and nations. An entire nation may repudiate God's laws. Even in such cases of wholesale rejection of God's laws, God exercises the margin of mercy.

God exercises the margin of mercy through the medium of flexibility. In many cases, God's justice is delayed. God's Mercy interposes a period (*heen*) between the violation and its desert,[59] providing a temporal opportunity for the perpetrator to reflect upon wrongdoing and its effects on others and the wrongdoer. Hard-hearted wrongdoers may misinterpret delayed justice to infer that no God exists, or they may mock God's lawlessness.[60] Even victims of wrongdoing may similarly conclude that God's justice is non-existent or uncertain. For persons of faith, however, whether they are perpetrators or victims of wrongdoing, God's flextime in rendering justice and practicing mercy furnishes an opportunity to make and receive amends, to seek and offer forgiveness. Delayed justice offers self-correction and healing. The margin of mercy is granted, says the Qur'an, "so that if any of you commits a bad deed out of ignorance, and after that repents and lives righteously, God is indeed forgiving and merciful."[61]

In an apparent contradiction to mercy-mingled flextime, the Qur'an invokes God's swift justice to affirm the adage that justice delayed is justice denied. The Qur'an frequently reminds the readers that "God is swift in reckoning."[62] Here, swiftness means that God is both accurate and prompt in dispensing justice. In common parlance, the notions of justice and accountability lose significance when wrongdoers are not swiftly or accurately punished, or good deeds remain unrecognized for long periods. However, God's justice is done either in this world or in the next. "And whoever desires a reward in (this) world, We shall give him of it; and whoever desires a reward in the Hereafter, We shall give him thereof."[63] The Day of Judgment (*yawm al-qiyamati*), a day when human beings will be gathered and held accountable for their deeds and misdeeds, says the Qur'an, is beyond doubt.[64] If justice is postponed to the Hereafter, the Qur'an assures that justice will be done accurately. "That Day will every soul be requited for what it earned; no injustice will there be that Day, for God is swift in taking account."[65] Here, swiftness means accurate.

By combining swift justice with the margin of mercy, the Qur'an is constructing a sophisticated framework that blends various competing values. Justice, mercy, accuracy, promptness, accountability, repentance, forgiveness, these and other competing values are not easily reconcilable. A reductionist legal system that discards some competing values in favor of others might be simpler to understand but remains unsatisfactory. However, a sophisticated legal system interweaves competing values into a complex synthesis. God grants flextime to wrongdoers to review and reform their impugned behavior. God grants flextime to victims to exercise patience and forgiveness. If the wrongdoer's reformation or the victim's forgiveness does not come forth, God administers true justice.

# Chapter 2

## Temporal Flexibility

This section delineates temporal flexibility under the Basic Code. Islam rejects the pre-Islamic belief that an idol of time (*al-ddahr*) has the inherent power to influence human life. By rejecting fatalistic temporality, Islam frees human beings from temporal captivity and thus introduces freedom and liberty to human understandings of time. Islam also repudiates anthropocentric notions of time, challenging the belief that human beings control time. Time is not a force to be mastered but a standard of measurement to be understood. Offering time as a rational but flexible tool for measuring durations and organizing and memorializing human affairs, Islam introduces the notion of temporal flexibility.

### A. Fatalistic Temporality

Flexibility rejects fatalistic temporality. Since time immemorial, fatalistic notions of time have preoccupied and distressed the human species. *Al-ddahr* was a pre-Islamic deity of temporality believed to bring life, death, happiness, and misery to human life.[66] In the pre-Islamic era, the inhabitants of Arabia

25

blamed *al-ddahr* if an affliction, calamity, or disaster struck them. Even in our times, the people espouse fatalistic views of time, as if time is a mighty power in its own right.[67] The Qur'an captures the fatalistic misunderstandings of time in the following words: "And yet they say: 'There is nothing beyond our life in this world. We die as we come to life, and nothing but *al-ddahr* destroys us.'"[68] The Qur'an rejects temporal fatalism, explaining that any notion of deistic temporality is speculative, not founded on any verifiable knowledge.[69] Time is not a god or goddess. Time has no deistic powers.

Time, like everything else, is God's creation. However, the Qur'an does not discard the notion of *al-ddahr* but transforms its meaning to describe eternity. However, *al-ddahr*, as a notion of eternity, has no power over the creation or extinction of human life. Nor does *al-ddahr* as a notion of eternity have any power to make human beings happy or miserable. The Qur'an rejects the notion of al-ddahr explicitly as a formidable force in its own right that determines human life.[70] According to the Prophet, God, and not eternity, creates and destroys all forms of life, including human beings.[71] The Qur'an clarifies this point even more clearly: "O Prophet, say to them, "It is God Who gives you life, then He is Who causes your death, then He is Who will gather you together on the Day of Resurrection, which is sure to come, but most people do not know."[72] God, not *al-ddahr*, rewards and punishes human beings for their conduct. Thus, Islam liberates human beings from the fatalistic notion of *al-ddahr*.

The Qur'an distinguishes between duration and eternity to explain flexible temporality.[73] The word *heen* designates duration, that is, a quantifiable but flexible period.[74] The word *al-ddahr* denotes eternity, that is, time that cannot be quantified.[75] The *heen* is a flexible period during which an event occurs. For example, human beings have been given the means of sustenance and dwelling on the earth for a while (*heen*),[76] suggesting that human habitation of the earth is not eternal. Likewise, the Qur'an instructed the believers not to ask for rules on certain matters during the period (*heen*) the Qur'an was being revealed, for, God might furnish stiff rules creating hardship.[77] The word *heen* in this verse implied that the Qur'an would be completed within a period, as it was in twenty-two years.

The *heen* as a flexible tool of temporality used to initiate, record, execute, perform, and extinguish human activity including legal obligations.[78] The *heen* does not imply that we always know in advance the exact duration of time in which an event would be completed. However, *heen* does signify a quantifiable period, which may or may not be ascertainable in advance or at all. Thus, how long human beings will dwell on earth is a period (*heen*), although its exact length is unknowable in advance. On the other hand, the tenure of a political office, such as that of the President, might be fixed for an ascertainable period.

In studying flexible temporality, it is imperative to bear in mind that time is correlated with the change, but time does not cause change. Time is a flexible yardstick, a standard, and a means of measuring change caused by other factors. Take the parable of a barren rock covered with mud.[79] The sweeping pressure of a rainstorm washes away the mud, and the rock can no longer hide its barrenness. The mud-covered rock before the rainstorm and the bare rock after the rainstorm display the change in the surface of the rock. Before and after the rainstorm are useful temporal points ($t_1$ and $t_2$) to observe the change in the rock. It is, however, the rainstorm and not time that removes the mud from the face of the rock and unveils its hardness.

Change is a widespread phenomenon in and around human life. Individuals and communities undergo and seek change. Phenomenal change reaffirms that the cosmos is inherently flexible and fluid. Nations rise to prominence and decay, just as individuals do. The formidable nations of 'Aad and Thamud faced destruction, a fact evident, says the Qur'an, from the ruins of their buildings.[80] In all cases of change, small and big, good and bad, time is a flexible tool to measure the change and the duration in which the change was completed. This emphasis away from time as a causative or determinative agent repudiates the notion of temporal fatalism, sending a powerful message that human beings are free to shape their destiny.

## B. Anthropocentric Temporality

Flexibility also repudiates anthropocentric temporality. Liberation from fatalistic temporality (that the vengeful deity of *al-ddahr* signifies) might embolden believers to suppose that they exercise sovereignty over time. Islam rejects anthropocentric notions of time, including notions such as that temporality and humanity, are coterminous, that time was created at the birth of humanity, or that humanity may control time. Philosophers, scientists, and others have been striving hard to answer the question that Aristotle asked: "In what sense if any, can time be said to exist?"[81] The Qur'an poses a different question to clarify that human beings have no control over time: "Has there not been a period (*heen*) within eternity (*al-ddahr*) during which man was nothing?"[82] This conception of eternity precedes the creation of human species and, therefore, time cannot be measured from the origin of human species. The human species has been granted only limited time (*heen*) within eternity. This view means that time will not end with the extinction of human species. This view of temporality is also consistent with the Islamic belief of the afterlife when human beings would be resurrected and held responsible for their deeds in the earthly life.[83]

Most interpreters of the Qur'an agree that according to the Qur'an, human beings do not control the natural signifiers of temporality, that is, sun and moon.[84] The keyword of the Qur'an that needs interpretation is *sakhkhar*.[85] Yusuf Ali, a mathematician by profession, and whose interpretation of the Qur'an is widely read in the English speaking world, including the United States, translates the word *sakhkhar* as "subject to you (human beings)."[86] Yusuf Ali translates an important verse of temporality as follows: "God has made subject to you sun and moon, both diligently pursuing their courses; and the day and the night He has (also) made subject to you."[87] However, Muhammad Asad, a Muslim convert from Judaism, translates *sakhkhar* to mean that sun, moon, day, and night, all are subservient to God's laws and not subject to human beings as Yusuf Ali suggests.[88] Asad clarifies that the celestial bodies and natural phenomena are subject to God's Laws and not to man's laws. [89] Marmaduke Picktall, a Muslim convert from Christianity, also spurns the idea of the subjection of celestial objects to human beings and accordingly translates *sakhkhar* to mean that the vehicles of temporality have been placed in the "service" of human beings.[90]

Two influential Muslim jurists also understand the word *sakhkhar* in terms of service for, rather than subjection to, human beings. Ismail Ibn Kathir, a fourteenth-century Muslim jurist, whose interpretations of the Qur'an are widely read in the world, sees as a God's favor that He has made celestial bodies and natural phenomena for the service of human beings.[91] In explaining the word *sakhkhar*, Abul A'la Maududi, a renowned jurist of the twentieth century, questions the translation of *sakhkhar* as "subject to." This misinterpretation, says Maududi, leaves the impression as if 'the chief aim of the life of man is to bring the earth and heavens under his subjection."[92] Reaching the same conclusion as did Ibn Kathir, Maududi sees *sakhkhar* as the subjection of sun, moon, day, and night to God's laws and not to the will of human beings. If heavenly bodies and the day and night "had not been subjected to certain fixed laws, life could not have been possible, not to speak of civilized life!"[93]

In sum, Islam offers a conception of time that has no deistic power to influence human life or destiny. Nor do human beings have any control over the signifiers of temporality: sun and moon.[94] They cannot alter the notion of eternity, but they can understand time as a flexible tool. They can use time as a practical yardstick to measure change, schedule events, coordinate efforts, wake up and sleep, work and relax, operate machines, record the temporal sequence of historical events, structure transactions, and perform other tasks. In using the time for utilitarian purposes, human beings need not enslave themselves to temporality.

### C. Blending Precision with Flexibility

The following discussion shows that Islam adopts a notion of temporality that blends precision with flexibility. The Qur'an mentions the precision of temporality, but at the same time, Muslim religious events, such as the Hajj and the Eids, are structured around lunar months. The lunar calendar is much more flexible than the solar calendar, which is a remarkable human invention to obtain precision. Even though the solar calendar has been universally adopted, the question remains whether the lunar calendar continues to offer a unique form of flexibility to accommodate seasons and variations in festivities. Reliance on both solar and lunar calendars might offer a more rewarding conception of temporality.

The Qur'an prescribes the twelve months cycle as a divine decree, an integral part of the cosmic design underlying God's creation of heavens and the earth.[95] Although God's decree does not explicitly mention the solar or lunar cycle of twelve months, Muslims believe that the Qur'an refers to the lunar cycle. The lunar movements are apparent to the human eye since the moon undergoes a gradual but visible reduction and increase in size. The varying size of the moon provides a basis for developing the sense of the month, as the moon rotates from crescent to crescent. The easily observable rotation of the moon around the earth furnishes a vivid contrast to the abstract but mathematically knowable rotation of the earth around the sun.

In counting time, Muslims adopt the natural flexibility of lunar temporality.[96] According to the Qur'an, the new moon indicates the start of a new period.[97] The Islamic lunar calendar makes no artificial adjustments to construct a rigid conception of the year, a macro unit of periodicity, as do some other lunar calendars.[98] A lunar month is either 29 or 30 days, but never 31 days or 28 days, as are some months of the Gregorian calendar -- a solar calendar constructed to absorb the solar year of approximately 365 days fully.[99] The lunar temporality varies from region to region, and a new moon sighted in the United States, for example, may or may not be sighted in Saudi Arabia.[100] This variation in moon sighting makes it difficult for Muslims to celebrate religious holidays on the same day throughout the world.[101] Some Muslims question moon sighting as a method of determining the lunar calendar.[102] They prefer that moon movements be calculated astronomically and a calendar constructed in advance.

Historically and before the discovery of astronomical knowledge, the lunar month has been observational rather than astronomical. A Muslim community may use the sighting method or astronomical data to determine the start of a new lunar month. Regardless of the method of determining the new crescent, the lunar year of 12 months consists of 354 days, 11 days shorter than the solar year.[103] However, the observational calendar relies on actual moon sightings. It predicts no exact dates in advance since it remains uncertain whether a lunar month will be 29 days or 30 days. This uncertainty, however, does not prevent scheduling of events according to the lunar calendar. In a lunar calendar based on sighting, the day of the week becomes a more critical scheduling matrix rather than the date of the month.[104] The cycle of seven days is more specific than the varying cycle of a lunar month.

In one particularly revealing verse, the Qur'an mentions the functionalities of both the sun and the moon and refers to visible stages of the lunar motion to declare that God has created these functionalities to facilitate human learning in counting time and knowing mathematics.[105] The existence of the two cycles, the lunar and the solar, one visible and the other calculable, one seen without effort and the other knowable with mathematical knowledge, affirms the mysteries of God's universe and the multiple layers of temporality that coexist in harmony, not in tension, with each other. There is no reason for Muslims to reject the concept of a solar year.

First, flexible temporality embraces precision. Counting is reaffirmed because some verses highlight the mathematical precision (*hisaban*) with which sun and moon float in their respective orbits.[106] Counting is reliable because the Qur'an declares that "it is not permitted the sun to catch up with the moon, nor can the night outstrip the day. Each floats in its mathematically-determined orbit."[107] This precision of the movements of sun and moon is repeated a couple of times in the Qur'an to underscore the point (repetition is a teaching methodology that the Qur'an frequently employs). Another verse reminds the reader that "the sun and the moon follow courses (exactly) computed."[108] This reference to precise orbiting of the celestial bodies opens the door for constructing more reliable conceptions of temporality, including astronomical calendars, to manage life and record historical events.

Omar Khayyam (d. 1123), a great Persian poet, whose *Rubaiyat* (Quatrains) were first made popular by Edward Fitzgerald in the nineteenth century Western literary circles, constructed a credible solar calendar. Khayyam was a leading mathematician and astronomer of his times[109] His work in geometry was so far ahead of its time that it was not put to use until Rene Descartes relied on it in the 17th century France.[110] In 1079, the Seljuk king in Iran summoned a team of astronomers and mathematicians to construct a precise calendar, primarily for instituting a more reliable schedule of revenue collection.[111] According to one calculation, the Gregorian calendar is off by 26 seconds.[112] However, the Khayyam calendar constructs the year as 365 days, 5 hours, 49 minutes, and 5.5 seconds----a configuration that exceeds the exact year by only 19.5 seconds.[113] According to yet another calculation, the Khayyam calendar makes an error of one day in 3770 years, whereas the Gregorian calendar makes the same error in 3330 years.[114] Thus, the Khayyam calendar is comparatively more precise and much older than the Gregorian calendar that was implemented in 1582.[115] Khayyam noted his calendar in a quatrain.[116] The Khayyam calendar, however, failed to attract the Muslim imagination that continues to appreciate the flexibility and fluidity of the lunar year.

The movement of the earth around the sun produces seasons (winter, spring, summer, and fall) and renders the concept of cyclical time. In non-Islamic cultures and communities, the great festivals are frequently tied to seasons of the year, particularly summer. These festivals celebrate human instincts by loosening constraints. The people indulge in eating, drinking, singing, dancing, and gather for parades, fireworks, folk dances, and concerts.[117]

The lunar calendar is meta-seasonal. The lunar cycle does not coincide with the seasons that are naturally related to the solar year. The lunar month of Ramadhan, for example, is not tied to any one season, and over the years, it rotates from one season to the other. Some Western observers believe that this rotation of the month of Ramadhan "causes hardship when it comes in summer."

Similarly, the Haj, the Muslim pilgrimage to Makkah, is a fixed lunar event in that it falls on the tenth of the lunar month of *zil-hijja*. However, even this great event is tied to no particular season. The Islamic festivals, called *al-idan*, are fixed on the lunar calendar but not tied to seasons. Celebrated with piety, prayers, and charity, these festivals are tied to the two of the five pillars of Islam, the Ramdhan and the Hajj. Id-al-Fitr is celebrated at the completion of Ramadhan and id-al-Adha at the completion of Hajj.[118] These days of joy have their own separate identity and they are not tied to agriculture, wars, victories, ethnic or national pride,

36

saints or prophets, summer or fall. They follow the natural flexibility of lunar temporality.

## D. Numerical Flextime

Numericalization of temporality, which facilitates the counting of time, is an inevitable human need. The Qur'an endorses the numericalization of time in the following verse. "And We have made the night and day two signs, and We erased the sign of the night and made the sign of the day visible that you may seek bounty from your Lord and may know the number of years and the account [of time]. Moreover, everything We have set out in detail."[119] The Qur'an presents the day and night cycle as the basis for measuring time. Even though new digital inventions have refined the human sense of temporality, the day and night cycle remains a fundamental unit for counting the units of the week, the month, and the year. Years construct the concept of a century. At the micro-level, the day has been divided into hours, minutes, seconds, and milliseconds. Increasingly, micro numericalization of temporality has become an integral part of human civilization as modern machines and gadgets require digitized time coordination for efficient performance and production. The Qur'an indicates a micro time unit smaller than "the twinkling of the eye."[120] Islamic law is entirely consistent with the precise digitization of time into micro-units.

Numerous legal systems, including contemporary Islamic law, rely on the numericalization of time to allocate rights and obligations to individuals. Any person below the age of 18, regardless of his or her intellectual and spiritual maturity, may be defined as a child.[121] Some rights and liberties, such as the right to vote, granted to adults may be restricted or denied to numerically-defined children.[122] Children are legally disabled from entering contracts.[123] The right to drive a motor vehicle, or fly an aircraft, run for a political office, or hold a judicial office, each is linked to numerical age.[124] Likewise, the obligation to serve in the armed forces may be enforced upon reaching a specified numerical age.[125] Specific jobs may not be available for persons of a particular numerical old age.[126] Even though the numerical age has become an unacceptable basis for denying rights and liberties, social and cultural constructs continue to attach certain stereotypes to old age.

In another book, I presented the concept of time triggers to demonstrate how law uses numerical points in time to initiate or terminate legal events.[127]For example, the law may prescribe the 18th birthday as the point in time when a person will enjoy the right to get married. The 18th birthday is a time trigger that allocates the right to marriage. Likewise, the law may identify a time trigger to file an income tax return or begin to receive social security benefits. These time triggers are designed for administrative conveniences. Numerical time triggers, however, do not take into consideration the unique facts of a person. An 18-year-old person may or may not be ready to assume the obligations of a contract.

Flexibility principle is not opposed to establishing time triggers for the allocation of rights and obligations. However, a rigid numerical infrastructure appears to be incompatible with the inherent flexibility and fluidity with which Islam views human realities. For example, the Basic Code does not define childhood or adulthood in terms of numerical age. The Qur'an refers to the age of puberty (*balagha*) but without assigning any number at which puberty is obtained. For example, the Qur'an mandates that trustees allow the orphans to manage their property upon reaching the age of puberty.[128] The Qur'an furnishes a functional and not a numerical standard to test to the age of puberty. If a minor has acquired sound judgment, he or she has reached the age of puberty.[129] The functional test does not provide a single numerical test for all to pass into adulthood. It is a person-specific test.

The normal lifecycle, however, follows a bell-curve. The Qur'an captures the bell-curve in the following descriptive verse: "We created you from dust, then from a sperm-drop, then from a clinging clot, and then from a lump of flesh, formed and unformed - that We may show you. And We settle in the wombs whom We will for a specified term, then We bring you out as a child, and then [We develop you] that you may reach your [time of] maturity. And among you is he who is taken in [early] death, and among you is he who is returned to the most decrepit [old] age."[130] A normal lifecycle begins with a near-zero temporality.[131] On the left side of the bell curve, the individual gradually rises to the best of his or her physical and mental strengths, acquiring physical prowess, height, maturity, and understanding of the world, and reaches the top of the curve. On the right side of the bell curve, the process of weakening begins. The individual gradually loses physical strength and mental alertness; health fails, disease occupies the body, and the individual dies, reaching zero temporality. On both sides of the bell curve, time does not cause bodily changes. However, the growth and decay within a person's physical and mental life may be documented in a numerical age. The temporality of a normal lifecycle is measured in units of time, such as years and months. The normal lifecycle follows a familiar bell-curve pattern. Nevertheless, the flexibility principle recognizes that each lifecycle is unique with many nuances and variations.

While the numericalization of aging is useful for keeping social and personal records, the richness and diversity of life must not be reduced to mere numbers. In the United States, the law has rightfully abandoned the numerical age as a reliable marker for economic or work-related retirement - a move consistent with the flexibility principle.[132] There is no one magic number for entering or exiting an active life. Though aging is inevitable, the chronological age does not fully represent the reality of individual life. Even though the human life span has not dramatically increased, the attitude toward aging is undergoing a substantial transformation.[133] Happiness has little to do with numbers (age, wealth, or progeny), and persons who engage in righteous deeds and hope (creative enterprising) build satisfying lives.[134]

Mandatory retirement age practiced in some Muslim states violates the flexibility principle.[135]Discrimination based on age is one way to attack the mandatory retirement age.[136] However, even the age discrimination argument supposes that chronological age is far from an objective standard to force people out of work. Chronological age does not tell us whether a person has lost the ability or skills to perform the obligations of a job. The test ought to be functional rather than numerical. Very few people will continue to work if they are not doing satisfactory work. Terminating the services of a person who is not adequately doing his or her assigned job can occur at any age.[137] The presumption that it occurs at the age of 55, 65, or 75 is too raw and rough to pass as a legal standard. The flexibility principle teaches us that numerical age might be a useful bureaucratic standard for administrative convenience, but it is an insufficient criterion for mandatory retirement or allocation of other rights and obligations.[138]

# Chapter 3

## Performance Flexibility

Performance flexibility is a value incorporated in the basics of Islamic law. It is a vital part of the divine decree of *yus'r*. If circumstances do not allow the performance of an obligation on time, the flexibility principle allows the obligation to be performed later when hardship has eased. The Qur'an lays down the principle of performance flexibility in a specific verse: "And if someone is in hardship, then [let there be] postponement until [a time of] ease. But if you give [from your right as] charity, then it is better for you, if you only knew."[139]Note that the performance flexibility is available only if there is a hardship. The obligation must be performed as soon as the hardship has eased. If the hardship does not ease, and the obligation cannot be performed, the flexibility principle urges the obligee to release the performance of the obligation. For example, if a borrower cannot pay back the loan due to financial constraints, the creditor may extend the loan period. If the borrower's hardship persists, the creditor may convert the loan into charity.

The following analysis illustrates how the flexibility principle permeates sequential and contingent obligations. This analysis, though derived from the framework of mandatory daily prayers and fasting, is instructive for drafting and performing transactions involving various types of sequential and contingent obligations.

## A.  Sequential Obligations

The flexibility principle does not repudiate the notion of sequentiality in the performance of obligations. To fully understand the performance flexibility of Islamic law, a brief discussion of punctuality and sequentiality will be useful. Punctuality demands that obligations be fulfilled at the appointed time. Sequentiality demands that obligations be fulfilled in the order in which they are laid out for performance. Punctuality and sequentiality may arise from the requirements of law or contract. Take the example of daily five prayers that Muslims are obligated to perform every day. The Basic Code mandates that the believers say their prayers at the appointed time, thus promoting punctuality.[140]The Prophet's Sunnah instructs Muslims to say mandatory prayers at stated times.[141] The obligation to say five prayers each day at fixed times is a continuous obligation for Muslims until death.[142]

The prayer obligations are sequential. Each day, the five prayers are performed sequentially, one following the other.[143] The afternoon prayer (*dhur*) follows the morning prayer (*fajr*); the late afternoon prayer (*asr*) follows the afternoon prayer (*dhur*); the prayer at sunset (*maghrib*) follows the later afternoon prayer (*asr*), and the night prayer (*isha*) follows the prayer at sunset (*maghrib*).[144]

As a general principle, performance flexibility cannot be invoked to disturb the sequential order of multiple obligations. Theoretically, the five prayers could be said in the exact sequence but without saying them at their appointed time. Since each mandatory prayer is short, the five prayers can be sequentially said all at once in a few minutes at any time during the day. However, the Basic Code requires both sequence and punctuality in the performance of daily prayers. For example, the *fajr* prayer must be said before the sunrise, and the *dhur* prayer must not be said before noon. Each prayer has an appointed time. Thus the obligation of five prayers incorporates both sequentiality and punctuality. When the five prayers are offered at appointed times, their sequence is automatically observed.

Sequential obligations may or may not be contingent upon one another. The sequence of prayer obligations is not contingent in that each daily prayer carries its own obligation separate from other prayers. One may completely miss the *fajr* (morning) prayer, and yet one is obligated to say the *dhur*(afternoon)prayer. In this sense, the saying of *dhur* (afternoon) prayer is not contingent upon the saying of the *fajr* (morning) prayer. Likewise, one may offer the *fajr* prayer but not at the appointed time. This lack of punctuality concerning the *fajr* prayer does not disturb the punctual observance of the remaining four prayers. In the sequence of daily five prayers, each prayer is an independent and self-contained obligation.

Performance flexibility is also available in meeting the obligation of daily prayers. As a general principle, the five daily prayers are performed in congregations in mosques on scheduled times.[145] This preferred method of discharging prayer obligation, however, is not rigid or oppressive. It is flexible. If needed, Muslims can pray at home. Under compulsion and necessity, prayers may be performed later than appointed times. Women are exempt from prayers during menstruation.[146] Travelers may offer shortened prayers for more efficient use of time.[147]

Likewise, fasting prescribed for Muslims during the month of Ramadhan carries inherent flexibility, for according to the Qur'an, God burdens no soul beyond endurance. "Fasting is for a fixed number of days, but if any of you is ill or on a journey, the prescribed number (missed) should be made up in later days."[148] This concession is repeated twice in the Qur'an to underscore that Islamic obligations are infused with pragmatism and flexibility. Besides, pregnant and nursing mothers may postpone fasting and fulfill their obligation later. The Qur'an promotes performance flexibility on the ground that "God intends every facility for you; He does not want to put you to difficulties." [149]

Learning from the sequential logic contained in the performance of daily prayers and fasting, worldly transactions may be similarly structured. For example, a long-term loan may contain sequential obligations to pay a portion of the loan at the appointed time each month. The scheduled payments are made until the entire loan is paid off. The obligor is required to make each payment on time and maybe burdened with late fees and other penalties if the payment is not made on time. The acceptance of a late payment does not disturb the schedule of subsequent payments. A late payment, like a late prayer, may be made before the next scheduled payment is due. Even though God is most forgiving if a prayer is not offered on time, a lender may impose fines for late payment. A lender imbued with the flexibility principle may not impose any late fees or waive them if a payment is delayed for a valid reason. Under secular law, the entire loan may be accelerated and made payable on demand if a borrower completely disregards payment punctuality. Under the flexibility principle, deceleration rather than acceleration may be structured to grant relief to the borrower under distress.

## B. Contingent Obligations

Contingent obligations may be distinguished from sequential obligations. Unlike sequential obligations, contingent obligations are due upon the occurrence of specified events. A contingent obligation is linked to a qualifying event and remains dormant until the qualifying event activates the obligation. The examples of contingent obligations include the waiting period for widows and their maintenance after the husband's death.[150] The Qur'an mandates that a decedent's wife wait for four months and ten days, called the *iddat* before she can enter into another marriage.[151] "If any of you die and leave widows behind, they shall wait concerning themselves four months and ten days: When they have fulfilled their term, there is no blame on you if they dispose of themselves in a just and reasonable manner. And God is well acquainted with what ye do."[152] This obligatory waiting period for the widow is contingent upon the husband's death since it begins from the day the husband dies.[153] The prescribed waiting period is sufficient to determine any pregnancy upon the husband's death since the *iddat* period is roughly half of the average pregnancy. After the expiration of the waiting period, widows are free to contract another marriage.[154]

Flexibility may or may not be available to restructure contingent obligations. For example, a widow may undergo a pregnancy test to ascertain whether she is pregnant. If she is not pregnant, could she contract another marriage before the expiration of the *iddat*? If pregnancy were the sole rationale underlying the *iddat*, and if pregnancy could be ruled out with certainty, the argument for flextime makes sense. However, the *iddat* serves multiple purposes. It serves to show respect for the deceased, to honor the marriage, and to interpose a reasonable mourning period for the grieving family. That is why the *iddat* is prescribed even for older widows on menopause. The flexibility is also allowed in that a man may propose to marry the widow during the *iddat* period.

48

The Basic Code itself provides flexibility for some contingent obligations. For example, the Qur'an mandates that a dying husband leave a will providing maintenance for his widow for a minimal period of one year.[155] "(In the case of) those of you who are about to die and leave behind them wives, they should bequeath unto their wives a provision for the year without turning them out, but if they go out (of their own accord) there is no sin for you in that which they do of themselves within their rights. God is Mighty, Wise."[156] Note that one-year maintenance is a contingent obligation activated on the day of the husband's death and not from the day of the writing of the will. However, the rule is flexible since the widow may get married after the *iddat* but before the expiration of the maintenance period. The maintenance is terminated if the widow leaves the decedent's house or contracts another marriage.[157] Thus, flexibility permeates the maintenance rule.

In landlord-tenant relations, flextime is available to mitigate the tenant's hardships. In normal circumstances, the tenant must pay rent on time. However, the landlord is obligated under the divine decree of *yus'r* and the Qur'an's specific allowance for flextime performance to accept late payments without penalties and late fees. In some cases, an affluent landlord may forego rent for a while until the tenant's hardship is removed.

Performance flexibility granted in Islam, however, cannot be abused. Prayers cannot be postponed for frivolous reasons such as laziness, gossip, or fun. Feigned illness or traveling for the sole purpose of avoiding fasting is fraudulent behavior, not entitled to God's concession. Flextime does not repudiate appointments and schedules. Nor is it a license for anyone to come and leave the workplace at will. If anything, performance flexibility outlaws arbitrariness or chaos at the workplace. It is a discipline that employees choose for themselves, though with the consent of the employer, who must also be generous and understanding.

These examples are not exhaustive but illustrative to affirm that performance flexibility is a profound Islamic value that places obligations in the realm of facility, not difficulty. Muslims are comforted that developed countries are adopting flextime to achieve material success and promote agreeable working conditions. They must now consider how they can use this beneficial Islamic value. Unfortunately, respect for time in many Islamic countries borders on anarchy. Punctuality in official appointments and social gatherings is uncommon. Clocks and watches serve as ornaments rather than instruments of the time. Frustrated with constant delays at every turn of the day, some organizations want to impose rigid time-structures reinforced with penalties. The remedy, however, lies in turning towards performance flexibility.

## C. Slavery

The Basic Code does not proscribe slavery, nor does it endorse slavery.[158] The Basic Code adopts the flexibility principle that beseeches Muslims to free slaves. Freedom of slaves and their humane treatment under slavery are the guiding principles of the Basic Code. If a Muslim nation opts for the abolition of slavery, it does not violate the Basic Code. [159]Under the Basic Code, freeing a slave is an act of virtue, an act of charity, an act of mercy, and sometimes an obligation. Even though the slaves may be bought or sold, they do not lose their humanity and can never be treated as goats or camels.[160]Under no circumstances may a Muslim treat slaves with cruelty or hard-heartedness. Physical beatings, withholding food, forcibly separating the members of a slave family, all such mistreatments are strictly prohibited under the Basic Code. The principle of convenience employed for the benefit of slaves is as vibrant as it is in every other aspect of Muslim life.

The Qur'an undermines classical slavery that existed in pre-Islamic times by adopting a rule of preference; the Qur'an states that a believing slave woman is better than a pagan free woman and, therefore, Muslim men should marry believing slave women rather than pagan free women, even though pagan free women might be more attractive.[161] The Qur'an offers a similar rule of preference to Muslim women, asking them to prefer Muslim slave men over pagan free men, even though pagan free men might be more glamorous.[162]Thus, the charm and glamor of a free person lose out to the slave's faith in Islam. Faith trumps freedom, and a believing slave is made superior to a non-believing free person.

The Basic Code provides numerous incentives for Muslims to free slaves. Whoever frees a Muslim slave will be protected from hellfire.[163] In order to strengthen the law of manumission, the Prophet laid a rule that if a Muslim manumits his or her share in a slave held in partnership with others, the Muslim, if he or she has sufficient means, is obligated to pay off his or her partners to buy complete freedom for the slave.[164]

The Qur'an requires the freedom of a believing slave in two cases. First, if a believer kills another believer by mistake, the killer is obligated to free a believing slave and pay compensation to the deceased's family.[165] This rule, however, is made flexible to the extent that if the killer does not have the means to pay compensation, the killer is obligated to fast for two consecutive months.[166]Second, freeing a believing slave is mandatory when a man divorces his wife by *zihar* and later retracts his words.[167] This rule is also made flexible to the extent that if the man engaged in *zihar* does not have the resources to obtain the freedom of a believing slave is obligated to fast for two consecutive months.[168]

Slavery under Islam acquires a unique status of equality, minimizing the difference between slave and slave-owners. The following hadith captures the principle of equality that the Prophet required Muslims to observe.

Narrated Al-Ma'rur: At Ar-Rabadha I met Abu Dhar who was wearing a cloak, and his slave, too, was wearing a similar one. I

52

asked about the reason for it. He replied, "I abused a person by calling his mother with bad names." The Prophet said to me, 'O Abu Dhar! Did you abuse him by calling his mother with bad names You still have some characteristics of ignorance? Your slaves are your brothers and Allah has put them under your command. So whoever has a brother under his command should feed him of what he eats and dress him of what he wears. Do not ask them (slaves) to do things beyond their capacity (power) and if you do so, then help them.'"[169]

The Prophet's Sunnah stated in the hadith above, clarifies three points. One, even cursing a slave and thus causing mental anguish, is prohibited, let alone engaging in mistreatment or cruelty toward slaves. Two, slave-owners are obligated to treat slaves as brothers and not as inferior servants. Slave-owners are not masters but protectors of slaves. As brothers, slaves are entitled to equal treatment. Slaves eat what owners eat; slaves wear what owners wear. Three, the principle of convenience applies to slaves. Slaves cannot be burdened with arduous work beyond their physical and mental tolerance. Owners must work with slaves if the work is too strenuous for the slaves to do it alone. It is unfortunate that some Muslims, particularly in the affluent parts of the Middle East, do not follow the Prophet's Sunnah and mistreat housemaids and male servants, the modern forms of slavery.[170]

# Chapter 4

## Diversity and Accommodations

The flexibility principle respects diversity and accommodation. A framework of diversity and accommodation presumes that each person has a unique set of strengths, talents, needs, and hardships and, therefore, all persons cannot be treated under one and the same rule. By contrast, a system prizing uniformity over diversity and parity over the accommodation is less likely to embrace normative flexibility. A framework of uniformity and parity presumes that equal treatment of diverse persons suppresses favoritism and generates fairness. Each framework carries elements of truth and each framework may potentially lead to abuses. Islamic law strikes a balance as it interweaves both frameworks recognizing uniformity, diversity, parity, and accommodation.[171]

In further deepening the concept of flexibility, the Qur'an recognizes that each person has a different capacity for bearing hardship. Some persons are sturdier than others. Law, therefore, cannot assume that all persons are equally equipped to carry the same burden. In recognizing the diverse range in personal capacities, the Qur'an makes two distinct arguments. First, the Qur'an recognizes that God does not burden a person beyond his or her capacity. "On no soul doth God place a burden greater than it can bear."[172] This revelation circumscribes the principle of parity reminding employers, educators, and others that individuals are designed for differing capacities and they cannot be fairly treated under one and the same standard. Second, the Qur'an instructs judges and administrators that they take into account each individual's exceptionality in rendering justice, enforcing accountability, and showing mercy and forgiveness: "Show forgiveness (with due regard for the person), enjoin what is good, and turn away from the ignorant (don't punish them)."[173] This verse has been interpreted to conclude that punishment cannot simply focus on the act of the perpetrator and ignore the person of the perpetrator.[174] Forgiveness, instruction, and punishment must be custom-designed following the capacities of the person in question.[175]

Even in allocating social goods, including education, jobs, and wages, and social respect, the flexibility principle requires that law accommodate persons with disabilities.[176] God admonished the Prophet of Islam when the Prophet turned his face away from a blind person, shunned him, and preferred to pay his whole attention to a pagan chieftain hoping that this influential man would embrace Islam.[177] Several verses of the Qur'an were revealed to protect the dignity of this person with a disability.[178] In our times, a new principle of emerging that law respect persons with disabilities. This accommodation is the founding principle of the Convention on Rights of Persons with Disabilities,[179] a global treaty that Muslims states have adopted in an overwhelming number.[180] The Convention urges signatory states to cultivate a culture that respects persons with disabilities, understands the difference as part of human diversity, and strives for the inclusion of persons with disabilities with equality of opportunity and without stigma or discrimination.[181]

# Chapter 5

## Creative Enterprising

Creative enterprising related to dreams and dreaming has a special significance in Islamic consciousness. Dreams are the perfect embodiment of flexible spatiotemporality. Dreams may interfuse past, present, and future temporalities, mixing events from the past with those in the future. The Qur'an, as well as the Prophet's Sunnah, affirms dreams and their interpretations.[182] Dreams could be false or true.[183] They may predict the future. Some dreams are tormenting.[184] Some are metaphorical. [185]Some are utterly meaningless.[186] For prophets, dreams are a source of God's revelations.[187] For example, the Prophet dreamt that he and his companions entered the holy places in the City of Makkah in safety, without fear, with their heads shaved or hair cut short. The dream came true when the Prophet conquered Makkah. The Qur'an affirmed the dream's veracity suggesting that God had forecast the events in the Prophet's mind through a dream.[188] On another occasion, the Prophet had dreamt that he would marry Aisha,[189] another dream that came true.

Dreaming demonstrates that the human mind's interior temporality is most flexible. The human mind carries the capacity to distinguish between past, present, and future. It understands cause and effect in the material world. However, in its world, the mind embraces a flexible conception of time, eschewing distinctions between past, present, and future. As noted above, dreams manifest complex temporality as events from different time zones are freely blended to plot new stories that cannot otherwise exist in the sequential material world. The blending of sequential temporalities does not occur in dreams only. The human mind, even in its most wakeful state, has an infinite capacity to imagine images and stories that cannot occur in the material world. In the mind's inner world, sequential temporality poses no barrier in creating fantastic visions and events taken from numerous zones of time and place.

Islam does not reject dreams as worthless. The Qur'an mentions several dreams that various prophets, kings, and even prison inmates had and sought their interpretations. These dreams defy the rational logic of the material world. For example, Abraham dreams that God is commanding him to sacrifice his son.[190] An Egyptian King dreams that seven lean cows devour seven fat cows.[191] A prison inmate dreams that he is carrying bread on his head and the birds are picking on the bread.[192] These dreams invite interpretation and force the interpreter to make sense of the dream. Abandoning a dream as useless nonsense is easy.[193]

The human mind's interior flexibility to manipulate time and place is conducive to imagination, creativity, and inventions. Dreams are possible because the mind (for example, that of Pablo Picasso) can freely mix and match times, objects, and places for creating fantastic combinations.[194] Friedrich August Kekule (1829-96), a leader in the history of organic chemistry, conceptualized the Benzene molecule structure after visioning in his dream a snake turning, twisting, and seizing its tail.[195] Creative artists, writers, and musicians have reported dreams as the source of new ideas. Dreaming is also a metaphor for imagining something beautiful or virtuous in the future. Many companies engaged in creative manufacturing let their inventors and research universities let their faculty work in complete freedom from anywhere, anytime.

Creativity, much like the interpretation of dreams, is a phenomenon of making sense out of the unfamiliar and out of what appears to defy common sense. Creativity is vigorous when the cognitive framework does not submit to any rigid or fixed notions of temporality. Respecting creativity in both real and metaphorical senses is an essential feature of the flexibility principle.

Historically, Islam-inspired creative enterprising entered all parts of an expanding Muslim empire. Poetry,[196] literature, mathematics,[197] navigation, and numerous other disciplines flourished as Muslims engaged in contemplation and reflection that the Qur'an repeatedly emphasizes.[198] Muslims absorbed and retooled the knowledge obtained from Babylon, Greece, Rome Persia, and India. Much of the creative enterprising had direct roots in the religion of Islam. Mathematics "was upgraded to calculate charity, inheritance, and taxes;" astronomy was retooled to accurately establish the direction of" Ka'ba and precise timings of prayers and fasting.[199]Navigational tools were developed to facilitate the pilgrimage to Makkah. This synergy between creativity and faith was a remarkable contribution to human civilization.

The most manifest creative enterprising took the form of Islamic architecture. The Dome of the Rock, a domed cylindrical core inserted in an octagonal framework with columns, arches, and fine handiwork, built in the seventh century, was a fusion of ideas borrowed from the Byzantine Empire and Persia.[200] The Alhambra in Grenada, Spain, complete in the fourteenth century, is a reflection of Paradise conceived in Islamic poetry.[201] The Taj Mahal, constructed in the seventeenth century, is a magnificent monument that a Muslim Emperor built for his wife who bore him fourteen children, but this architectural marvel displays the calligraphy of twenty-two passages and fourteen entire chapters from the Qur'an inlaid in black marble.[202]

Unfortunately, some Muslim states suppress individual creativity. Autocratic governments, particularly in the Arab Middle East, allocate significant state resources to preserving dynastic regimes and family rule. Consequently, the repressive state has little respect for freedom of speech, liberty of expression, artistic creativity, and research-based scientific discoveries. Many Muslim communities are functioning at a minimal level of creativity and invention. Muslims rarely win Nobel prizes in hard sciences. Poverty, mismanagement, and numerous other social ills infest

Muslim states. Creative enterprising has ceased to exist. For modernists, Islam has turned into a force of decadence. For Muslim fundamentalists, modern creativity has become synonymous with evil and deviation from Islamic ethos.

Islam does not oppose material prosperity. Unlike other religions that might preach asceticism, Islam is a religion of both the material and meta-material worlds. The good life, good health, clean communities, healthy foods, well-functioning cities, beautiful buildings, well-constructed highways, televisions, internet, computers, household gadgets of comfort and convenience, all are fully compatible with Islam as a vibrant faith. Islam does not favor poverty, sickness, dirty living conditions, primitiveness, ignorance, and harsh life without amenities. There is a reason why practicing Muslims prefer to live in prosperous communities, including Europe and North America. The reason is simple. They see no conflict between prosperity and faith or between freedom and faith.

The material decadence, irrational social and cultural barriers, and undemocratic political repression in Muslim states can be reversed if the flexibility principle is taken seriously. If Muslim men and women are allowed to express their talents and personal powers, Muslim states can overcome poverty, disease, and other social ills. If Muslims are allowed to choose rulers, political repression will be minimized. Creative enterprising cannot flourish if rulers are ruthless and intolerant of dissent. Nor can it flourish if the culture or community forces individuals to devote most of their time in performing religious rituals. The time devoted to spiritual life must be balanced against material pursuits. The material world cannot be sacrificed to obtain the benefits of the meta-material world. Islam teaches balance and flexibility, the paradigms that have been lost in the thicket of ignorance.

# Chapter 6

## Adaptable Normativity

This chapter introduces the concept of adaptable normativity to explain that Islamic divine law, revealed in the Qur'an and the Prophet's Sunnah, is not tied to any single spatiotemporality or any spatiotemporality at all. No tribe, culture, linguistic community, generation, or country can claim to command a superior knowledge of the Basic Code. The Qur'an and the Prophet's Sunnah are accessible to all Muslims of all generations, either personally or through the medium of teachers. Islam is not an Arab religion. Islam is a universal faith that repudiates racial, national, territorial, and linguistic boundaries. The access to the Basic Code is even more convenient now that the Qur'an and the Prophet's Sunnah have been translated into numerous languages.

Arabic, Persian, Urdu, Malay, Turkish, English, Spanish, and French are the languages of Islam. In addition to the Basic Code, Islamic legal literature is available in numerous national languages of Muslim States. Despite understanding the Basic Code in their own vernacular, however, Muslims of various linguistic traditions listen to the Qur'an in its revealed language and say the daily prayers in the revealed language. The revealed language of the Qur'an shall continue to illuminate the hearts of reciters and the ears of listeners but the meaning of the Qur'an and the Prophet's Sunnah are by no means confined to the Arabic language. This flexibility to understand the meaning of the Basic Code in any language and in all languages is the foundation of Islam's timeless universality.

We know that the Qur'an was revealed in the seventh century over a period of twenty-two years (610-632). Likewise, the Prophet's Sunnah is completed within the same period. The Qur'an and the Prophet's Sunnah, both divine sources, responded to the beliefs, laws, traditions, and customs of the seventh-century Arab pagans of Makkah and Jews of Medina. In this sense, the Basic Code is rooted in the social realities of seventh-century Arabia. If the Basic Code were a law exclusively for seventh-century Arabia, it would have little claim to guide the people of Persia, Mesopotamia, Egypt, India, Indonesia, Malaysia, sub-Saharan Africa, Europe, North America, and other regions. Likewise, what was relevant in the seventh century might be irrelevant in the twenty-first century. Following this line of argument, Islam is outdated and has little relevance to contemporary realities. Nevertheless, this line of argument is rarely accepted in the Muslim world.

According to Muslim beliefs, the Basic Code is timeless and relevant to the entire world. If so, the Basic Code cannot be confined to its seventh-century interpretations and understandings. The Qur'an itself states the Prophet has been sent as a mercy to the entire world.[203] In his last sermon, the Prophet urged the audience to reject preferences based on race and nationality, explaining that the Arab has no superiority over the non-Arab, and the non-Arab has no superiority over the Arab.[204] Likewise, Allah was not the God of anyone exclusive tribe or nation. Allah is the One God of all humanity, including Hindus, Buddhists, Jews, Christians, and even Pagans who do not believe in any God.[205] Anyone in the world can become Muslim with a simple declaration: God is one and Muhammad is His Prophet.[206]

Anyone, including non-Muslims, may read and seek guidance from the Qur'an and the Prophet's Sunnah. In Islam, nothing is hidden; there are no confidential scriptures; there is no clerical hierarchy; no permission of any jurist, Imam, or government is needed to embrace Islam. The universality of Islam is its defining attribute. The Qur'an, though revealed in Arabic, is meta-lingual. Arabs cannot claim to know Islam better than other Muslims. The Qur'an is easy to understand and prohibits complicated interpretations or innovative exegetical renderings.[207]

The Basic Code is non-amendable. However, even non-amendable texts are inevitably subject to temporal interpretations. Each generation of believers situated in a specified period receives eternal divine texts and understands them according to its capacities, including instincts, state of knowledge, cultural and moral development. Each generation learns from prior generations and may respect prior interpretations just as judges respect prior holdings. No one generation of believers, however, even if it is situated in close temporal proximity with the messenger, has a superior claim to know divine texts more than others. Since divine texts are universal, free of spatial and temporal confinements, each generation may in good faith interpret divine texts even if its interpretations differ from those of prior generations. This right of each generation to receive and interpret divine texts may be called adaptable normativity.[208]

In Islam, the law in the Qur'an is known as *Sunnat Allah* or God's Way.[209] The law of the Qur'an, however, is not something completely new. The law of the Qur'an is related to prior divine Law that has been delivered piecemeal over thousands of years to different nations through different prophets in different languages and under variant conditions of human life. These variations in the delivery of divine law do not affect the law's unity, integrity, coherence, or authenticity. According to Muslims' belief, the Qur'an is the final testament of divine law. Revelations previous to the Qur'an are parts of the divine law. The Qur'an itself mentions God's revelations to prophets preceding Prophet Muhammad, explicitly naming "Abraham, Isma'il, Isaac, Jacob, and the Tribes, Jesus, Job, Jonah, Aaron, Solomon, and David."[210]In addition to mentioning prophets, the Qur'an affirms the divine books in which these messages are collected, naming the Torah, the *Injeel* (New

68

Testament), and the *Zaboor* (Psalms).[211] Revelations to successive prophets constitute a series of divine texts affirming God's Way. The unity of divine law is assured because its author is the same God. The Mother Book, the original source, sublime, and full of wisdom, from which all revelations to all prophets are given, is secured in God's presence.[212]

According to believers, Islamic divine texts are immutable.[213] The immutability of divine texts may not be confused with God's immutability. God's immutability is not discussed here.[214] Islamic divine texts do not change with time. They are subject to no regression or progression. They do not deteriorate or improve with time. The divine texts can be set aside and not enforced. The people may separate the legal system from divine texts, as secular systems do. No exigencies, however, justify the reformation of divine texts wholly or partially. Divine law bears no relation to temporality. Divine Law does not exist in time or space. It has no past, present, or future. It is not tied to the earth, moon, sun, or any conception of spatiotemporality. Divine law cannot be made, modified, or repealed. Divine law is God's Will.

While divine texts are immutable for believers, their human reception is imperfect and therefore mutable. Reception is imperfect because human capacities, including instincts and knowledge, which grasp divine texts, are variant and imprecise. Instincts and knowledge are the primary human tools for understanding divine texts. Instincts embedded deep in our being illuminate divine law guide our survival. Knowledge, a special gift that Creator has bestowed upon humanity,[215] empowers individuals and nations in recognizing and obeying the divine law.[216] While human instincts might not alter from generation to generation, the state of knowledge does change. Each generation acquires knowledge but not the same knowledge. As knowledge varies, the understanding of divine texts varies. For example, the verse that 'sun and moon rotate in orbits or float in space'[217] makes a different sense to generations equipped with scientific knowledge. The generations that took sun and moon floating in the skies as poetic metaphors did not know planetary motion.[218]

It is doubtful whether divine texts can be interpreted through originalism, a methodology of interpretation anchored in fixed spatiotemporality. Originalism requires that a text be understood and applied according to its meaning at the time of its creation.[219] For example, originalism demands that the Eighth Amendment of the United States Constitution, which prohibits cruel and unusual punishment, be interpreted by assigning meaning to its phrases as understood at the time of its enactment, the year 1791.[220] Because the death penalty was not a cruel and unusual punishment in 1791, the originalists argue, the Eighth Amendment cannot be interpreted to outlaw capital punishment.[221]

While originalism may be applied to interpret human texts, it does not work to interpret divine texts. As noted above, the Qur'an was revealed in the seventh century over twenty-two years

(610-632). Originalism would demand that words of the Qur'an be assigned the same meaning as these words were understood in the early seventh century Arabia. This view of originalism is problematic because, according to Muslims, the Qur'an is the word of God and not the Prophet himself. It will be unacceptable, if not blasphemous, for jurists to engage in speculation over what God meant by choosing a specific word of the Qur'an. Since God revealed the Qur'an to the Prophet, another view of originalism may demand that words of the Qur'an be understood as the Prophet understood them. This view is credible to the extent that most Muslim jurists make a serious effort to reconcile words of the Qur'an with the sayings of the Prophet. In Islam, the Prophet's sayings are considered divine texts, though the sayings are not ranked as high as the Qur'an. Furthermore, there is a dispute over which of the Prophet's sayings are authentic, and which are fabricated. Therefore, if a Prophet's saying cannot be reconciled with the plain meaning of the Qur'an, the Qur'an overrules the Prophet's saying. Thus, originalism fails to solve difficult cases when the Qur'an and the Prophet's sayings are incompatible.

There are even more severe problems with applying originalism to divine texts. Since the Qur'an is universal, its meaning cannot be confined to seventh-century Arabia. The Qur'an as a book for the entire humanity of all times must make sense in the twenty-first century Arabia, in Indonesia, Nigeria, the United States, indeed in every part of the world in every century. If the Qur'an can only be understood by reference to linguistic conventions of the seventh-century Arabic, the Qur'an turns into a historical text meant for the Arabs of the seventh century. Conversely, since the Qur'an is indeed a universal and timeless divine text, for this is what the Muslims believe, its meaning cannot be confined to any one community, culture, or century, thus defeating the argument central to the maintenance of originalism as interpretive methodology.

In contrast to originalism, adaptable normativity safeguards the universality and timelessness of divine texts. Each generation of believers is free to interpret divine texts in light of its wisdom. This freedom is not confined to interpretations. Nations may exercise their freedom in submission to God or rejection of God. They may embrace or repudiate divine texts. This extensive freedom is part of God's plan. The Qur'an is crystal clear on this point. "The guiding of the people is not your duty (O Prophet); God guides whom He wills."[222] When exercised in submission, human efforts to understand divine law bear fruit. When exercised in rejection, human freedom loses God's Way and divine law becomes increasingly inaccessible. "And had God willed, He could have made you (all) one nation, but He sends astray whom He wills and guides whom He wills. But you shall certainly be called to account for what you used to do."[223] It appears that each generation is under an obligation to draw guidance from divine texts, for it will be held accountable for its applications of divine law. No generation can rely on interpretations and applications of prior generations to escape its efforts to contemporize divine texts.

Adaptable normativity is compatible with the flexibility principle. It allows each generation of believers to seek guidance from divine texts as if these texts are revealed just for that particular generation. Each generation of believers may benefit from prior understandings of divine texts. Previous understandings of divine texts cannot be discarded on the simple basis that prior interpretations are old or belong to another culture or socio-economic realities. Each generation of believers must make a serious and sincere effort to incorporate prior understandings into their understandings of divine texts.[224] There is no harm in embracing a presumption that a prior understanding of divine texts is valid and enforceable, and any deviation from a prior understanding requires rigorous reconsideration and the burden is on the nation and jurists who propose to deviate from a prior understanding.[225] Once this burden is met, a new understanding of the divine texts replaces a prior understanding. This presumptive methodology is not only fully compatible with the flexible principle but it also assures continuity.

Adaptable normativity also allows the flourishing of various schools of jurisprudence, just as various schools of jurisprudence flourished in the classical period.[226] Since now the Muslim world is divided into communities and states, each community and state may have its interpretations of the divine texts.[227] The culture, socioeconomic realities, language, local customs, political system, and history of Malaysia, for example, shares little in common with the culture, socioeconomic realities, language, local customs, political system, and history of the United Arab Emirates (UAE).[228] These nations are actively engaged in Islamic financing, but they launch modern financial instruments with differing understandings of Islamic law.[229] Neither Malaysia and nor the UAE can claim that its financial instruments are more Islamic because it has a better understanding of Islam. The flexibility principle will allow both Malaysia and the UAE the freedom to interpret divine texts for the launching of financial instruments.[230]

Adaptable normativity does not threaten the unity of Islam. There is enough in creed and practice of Islam that unifies the Muslim world. All Muslims believe that the Qur'an is the word of God. All Muslims believe in the ministry of the Prophet Muhammad. All Muslims believe in the five foundational behaviors, even when they fail to practice: (1) the belief in One God and Muhammad as God's messenger; (2) the obligation of saying daily prayers; (3) fasting in the month of Ramadhan; (4) giving zakat on surplus resources; (5) and making a pilgrimage (hajj) once in lifetime if affordable. These commonalities define the core values of Islam.[231]Beyond these core values, law-abiding Muslims will differ over a thousand points. Their difference over points of law does not weaken Islam as a religion or as a body of law. Any group, community, or nation that strives to impose its own particularized understanding of Islam over others, mainly through coercion or violence, is misguided.

# Conclusion

The Islamic flexibility principle is rooted in the divine decree of *yus'r* (convenience). Convenience rather than hardship defines the social organization and transactional relations. Flexibility principle instructs lenders, landlords, employers, and others who occupy positions of power to furnish convenient contracts to borrowers, tenants, employees, and other obligors. Furthermore, the flexibility principle endorses legal minimalism in the application punishments prescribed in the Basic Code. Legal minimalism maximizes the freedom of individuals and communities to negotiate transactions without over-regulation. Temporal flexibility is compatible with contemporary notions of flextime and flex-place, discarding thoughtless restrictions on the workplace. However, temporal flexibility does not repudiate the notions of time and place commitments critical to the performance of obligations. The flexibility principle supports creative enterprising, as it establishes a mindset that can breathe freely without too many restrictions.

Finally, the flexibility principle allows a dynamic jurisprudence in consonance with changing social and economic realities. Previous understandings of the Basic Code must be respected but not blindly followed. Since the Basic Code is universal and timeless, each generation of jurists and believers may read and interpret the Qur'an and the Prophet's Sunnah. The flexibility principle is a jurisprudential gift for all legal systems of the world. Lawyers, jurists, and judges across legal traditions may benefit from its core meaning. The book recommends that Muslim states incorporate the flexibility principle in their modern legislation and the laws they borrow from civil and common law traditions.

---

# Endnotes

[1] The phrase, the Basic Code, consisting of the Qur'an and the Prophet's Sunnah, was first introduced in the following article: Ali Khan, *The Reopening of the Islamic Code: The Second Era of Ijtihad*, 1 UNIV. ST. THOMAS L. J. 341 (2003). The Qur'an is the supreme text of law. According to Muslims, the Qur'an is the word of God revealed to the Prophet Muhammad (peace be upon him). The Prophet's Sunnah is the case law that the Prophet rendered during his life. The Prophet's Sunnah is derived from his sayings, acts, and his commentaries on the Qur'an. The Prophet's sayings are available in various collections. Sahih Bukhari and Sahih Muslim are two such collections that Sunni Muslims regard as most reliable. Other compilations that the Sunnis favor are Sunun Abu Dawud, Sunun Nisai, Tirmidhi, Malik's Muwatta. Each collection is named after the name of the collector. Shia jurists rely on their own compilations. Sunni and Sunnah should not be confused with each other. Sunni and Shia are the sects of Islam. Sunnah means the way, the law. The Prophet's Sunnah means the Prophet's way or the Prophet's law. Both Sunni and Shia sects believe in the Prophet's Sunnah, but rely on different collections of the Prophet's authentic sayings.

[2] The word *yus'r* is a noun derived from the tri-literal root of *ya, sin, ra*. Forty-four verbs, nouns, adjectives, and nominals derived from this root occur in the QUR'AN.

[3] Commentators recognize Islam's influence on the English Common Law. "In 1955, Henry Cattan noted that the English trust closely resembled and probably derived from the earlier Islamic institution of *waqf*. George Makdisi revealed many parallel institutions in Islamic and western legal education, including most notably the scholastic method, the license to teach, and the law schools known as Inns of Court in England and madrasas in Islam. Abraham Udovitch pointed out that the European *commenda* probably originated from Islam" *See* John A. Makdisi, *The Islamic Origins of the Common Law*, 77 N.C.L. Rev. 1635, 1639-1640 (1999).

[4] Majid Khadduri & Herbert J. Liebesny, ORIGIN AND DEVELOPMENT OF ISLAMIC LAW 81-84 (The Lawbook Exchange Ltd., 1955)(describing the incorporation of European civil codes in modern legal systems of Muslim states).

[5] QUR'AN, sura al-Qamar 54:17.

[6] Liaquat Ali Khan, *The Immutability of Divine Texts*, 2008 BYU L. Rev. 807 (2008).

[7] QUR'AN, sura al-Baqara 2: 185.

[8] QUR'AN, sura al-Kahf 18:88.

[9] QUR'AN, sura ash-Shar 18:88.

[10] SAHIH BUKHARI, Bk# 4, Hadith # 219.

[11] SAHIH BUKHARI, Bk# 2, Hadith # 19.

[12] On one occasion, a Bedouin stood up and started urinating in the Prophet's mosque while the Prophet was present in the mosque. The Muslims in the mosque were outraged. They caught the Bedouin and were about to beat him up when the Prophet intervened and instructed them not to harm the Bedouin. The Prophet asked the attendees to pour a bucket of water over the place where the Bedouin had passed the urine. SAHIH BUKHARI Bk.# 73, Hadith # 176.

[13] It has been narrated on the authority of Abu Masa that when the Messenger of Allah deputed any of his Companions on a mission, he would say: Give tidings (to the people); do not create (in their minds) aversion (towards religion); show them leniency and do not be hard upon them. SAHIH MUSLIM, Bk #19, Hadith #4297.

[14] In the United States, for example, courts may refuse to accept a mechanical application of a statute that produces an absurd result. *See for example*, State v. Delaurier, 488 A.2d 688, 694 (R.I. 1985).

[15] Commenting upon the Equal Protection of Laws, the United States Supreme Court recognizes that equality is available to "all persons similarly circumstanced." F. S. Royster Guano Co. v. Virginia, 253 U. S. 412, 415 (1920)."

[16] Tigner v. Texas, 310 U. S. 141, 147 (1940).

[17] QUR'AN, sura al-Baqara 2:286.

[18] Flexibility principle is also conducive to living a spiritual and contemplative life. Modern life conducted under precise temporality and rigid obligations is highly stressful; it disables the person from experiencing meditative contentment that comes from a relaxed mindset and serene surroundings. Islamic life shuns crass materialism, self-destructive competition, and cutthroat rush toward achieving power, money, and social status. Accordingly, Islamic spirituality is sustainable with the flexibility principle. God admonished even the Prophet Muhammad when the Prophet showed haste-prone eagerness to receive revelation. QUR'AN, sura Qiyamah 75:16

[19] Black's Law Dictionary (arbitrariness is defined as individual discretion founded on prejudice or preference rather than on reason or fact.)

[20] For example, the highway patrol may not sufficient officers to stop and issue speeding ticket to every driver found speeding. But even in such cases, rule enforcement may lead to racial or gender discrimination.

[21] The Prophet encouraged Imams to act justly. Narrated Abu Huraira: If the Imam orders people with righteousness and rules justly, then he will be rewarded for that, and if he does the opposite, he will be responsible for that." SAHIH BUKHARI, Bk. #52, Hadith # 204

[22] Narrated Al-Azraq bin Qais: We were in the city of Al-Ahwaz on the bank of a river which had dried up. Then Abu Barza Al-Aslami came riding a horse and he started praying and let his horse loose. The horse ran away, so Abu Barza interrupted his prayer and went after the horse till he caught it and brought it, and then he offered his prayer. There was a man amongst us who was (from the Khawari) having a different opinion. He came saying. "Look at this old man! He left his prayer because of a horse." On that Abu Barza came to us and said, "Since the time I left Allah's Apostle, nobody has admonished me; My house is very far from this place, and if I had carried on praying and left my horse, I could not have reached my house till night." Then Abu Barza mentioned that he had been in the company of the Prophet, and that he had seen his leniency. SAHIH BUKHARI, Bk #73, Hadith #148.

[23] Narrated Abu Huraira: The Prophet said, "The signs of a hypocrite are three: 1. Whenever he speaks, he tells a lie. 2. Whenever he promises, he always breaks it (his promise ). 3. If you trust him, he proves to be dishonest. (If you keep something as a trust with him, he will not return it.)" SAHIH BUKHARI, Bk #2, Hadith #32.

[24] Christian Avery & Diane Zabel, THE FLEXIBLE WORKPLACE 5 (Greenwood, 2001)(the generic term of flextime for work schedules that permit flexible starting and quitting times originated in West Germany).

[25] However, alternative work arrangements do not relieve employers of their legal obligations. For more on employer obligations *see* Pamela V. Rothenberg, Alternative work schedules: Employers Benefit when Employees Have Choices, JOURNAL OF PROPERTY MANAGEMENT (Jan.-Feb.(2006)

[26] The concept of flex-place benefits the health of employees. Joanne Bushell, Regus vice president for the Middle East and Africa said, "Lack of sleep is clearly detrimental to health and happiness. Long working hours are closely linked to heart disease" According to Bushell, "allowing employees to work closer to home can have an important impact on family life and provide workers with a few more minutes' sleep each morning" *See* Abeer Mogeem & Jet Van Eeghen, *Flexible work schemes could help sleep-starved Kingdom workers*, Arab News (14 February 2013).

[27] Emory University, for example, explains several benefits of flexible workplace. Among other benefits, flexible workplace expands labor pool geographically, reduces or eliminates commute and decreases work-related expenses. http://www.worklife.emory.edu/workplaceflexibility/quickguides/options.html

[28] Though the term legal minimalism is a contemporary term, the concept is not new. Al-Haramayn al-Juwayni, a Muslim jurist of the eleventh century, articulated a concept similar to Islamic legal minimalism. *See* Intisar Rabb, *Islamic Legal Minimalism: Legal Maxims and Lawmaking When Jurists Disappear in* LAW AND TRADITION IN CLASSICAL ISLAMIC THOUGHT 146 (Palgrave Macmillan, 2013).

[29] QUR'AN, Sura al Ma'ida 5:101.

[30] SAHIH BUKHARI, Bk # 60 Hadith # 1

[31] Narrated Ibn Abbas: Some people were asking Allah's Apostle questions mockingly. A man would say, "Who is my father?" Another man whose she-camel had gone astray would say, "Where is my she-camel? "So Allah revealed this Verse in this connection: "O you who believe! Ask not about things which, if made plain to you, may cause you trouble." SAHIH BUKHARI, Bk # 60 Hadith # 146.

[32] SAHIH BUKHARI, Bk # 75   Hadith # 373.

[33] Narrated 'Abdullah bin 'Amr : Allah's Apostle stopped (for a while near the Jimar at Mina) during his last Hajj and the people started asking him questions. A man said, "Ignorantly I got my head shaved before slaughtering." The Prophet replied, "Slaughter (now) and there is no harm in it." Another man said, "Unknowingly I slaughtered the Hadi before doing the Rami." The Prophet said, "Do Rami now and there is no harm in it." So, on that day, when the Prophet was asked about anything (about the ceremonies of Hajj) done before or after (its stated time) his reply was, "Do it (now) and there is no harm."SAHIH BUKHARI, Bk. # 26, Hadith No. 792.

[34] QUR'AN, sura al-Isra 17:32.

[35] QUR'AN, sura al Noor 24:2.

[36] SAHIH BUKHARI, Bk # 82 Hadith # 806; SAHIH MUSLIM, Bk # 17   Hadith # 4192; SUNAN ABUDAWD, Bk # 38  Hadith # 4435.

[37] Jabir b. Samura reported: As he was being brought to Allah's Apostle I saw Ma'iz b. Malik-a short-statured person with strong sinews, having no cloak around him. He bore witness against his own self four times that he had committed adultery, whereupon Allah's Messenger said: Perhaps (you kissed her or embraced her). He said: No. by God, one deviating (from the path of virtue) has committed adultery. He then got him stoned (to death).  SAHIH MUSLIM, Bk # 17, Hadith # 4198.

[38] Id.

[39] Abu Huraira reported Allah's Apostle  as saying: Verily Allah has fixed the very portion of adultery which a man will indulge in, and which he of necessity must commit. The adultery of the eye is the lustful look, and the adultery of the tongue is the licentious speech, the heart desires and yearns, which the parts may or may not put into effect. SAHIH MUSLIM, Bk #33, Hadith #6421.

[40] SAHIH MUSLIM, Bk # 17, Hadith # 4196.

[41] Id.

[42] QUR'AN, sura al-Nisa 24:4. In light of high proof, one might conclude that the offense of *zina* is aimed at discouraging public nudity rather than unlawful sexuality in privacy.

[43] Id. 24:5.

[44] In my Islamic Law class at Washburn University School of Law, students pose the following question: What is the point in prohibiting *zina* if so many escape routes have been built to avoid the prescribed punishment? In answering this question, I emphasize the varying mindset toward secular law and divine law. With respect to secular law, existing escape routes are exploited and new escape routes are created to avoid punishment or other legal burdens, For example, tax shelters are escape routes to avoid the payment of taxes. With respect to divine law, however, the mindset is not the same. The believers do not wish to find an escape route to dodge God's law. The believers obey divine law to please God and not to simply avoid payments. This distinction explains why some new Muslims would continue to confess the offense of *zina*, even though they knew the harsh punishment that would follow. Islamic criminal law is founded on a simple paradigm: Harsh punishments demonstrate how much God dislikes the offenses even though God draws no pleasure in inflicting punishment for these offenses.

[45] Art. 1, Sec. 9. This constitutional provision was made to deviate from the common law tradition that did not prohibit ex post facto laws. *See* John S. Gibson, DICTIONARY OF HUMAN RIGHTS LAWS 111 (Scarecrow Press, 1996). Nuremberg trials of Nazis were conducted by disregarding the jurisprudence of ex post facto laws. *See* Kingsley Chiedu Moghalu, GLOBAL JUSTICE: THE POLITICS OF WAR CRIMES TRIALS 37 (Greenwood, 2006).

[46] QUR'AN, sura al-Baqara 2:242.

[47] The concepts of force majeure and act of God are rules of flexibility derived from necessity. "It is a well-settled rule of law, that if a party by his contract charge himself with an obligation possible to be performed, he must make it good, unless its performance is rendered impossible by the act of God . . ." Dermott v. Jones, 69 U.S.1, at 7 (1965).

[48] Here the concept of circumstantial exception is not synonymous with ordinary exceptions. Circumstantial exceptions suspend the rule under exceptional circumstances. For example, certain human rights, such as the right to vote, may be suspended under special circumstances like epidemics. *See* International Covenant on Civil and Political Rights, Art. 4(a).

[49] QUR'AN Sura Al-Baqara 2:173.

[50] QUR'AN Sura al-An'am 6:119.

[51] There are four verses of the QUR'AN containing the word *qisas*. Sura al-Baqara 2:178; 2-179; 2:194. Sura al-Ma'idah 5:45. Qisas is also translated as law of equality and retaliation.

[52] Other classifications of crimes are known as hadud (crimes for which punishment is prescribed in the Basic Code), and ta'zir (most crimes that the state can formulate and punish).

[53] *See*, for example, The Iranian Penal Code, Art. 689 (1996).

[54] QUR'AN, Sura al-Baqara 2:178 (trans. Muhsin Khan).

[55] British Broadcasting Corporation, Iranian Sentenced to Blinding for Acid Attack Pardoned (July 31, 2011).

[56] The word mercy in its various derivatives is mentioned over 300 times in the QUR'AN.

[57] QUR'AN, sura al an'am 6:12.

[58] QUR'AN, sura al-An'am 6:12; 6:54.

[59] God's margin of mercy is not unique to Islam. It is recognized in other faith systems as well. *See*, for example, *Ezek*. 7:27.

[60] QUR'AN, sura Yunus 10:21. During the prophet's life, some disbelievers made fun of God if their wrongdoing was lightly punished, ridiculing that God's justice is short-lived.

[61] QUR'AN, sura al-An'am 6:54.


[62] QUR'AN, sura al-Baqara 2:202. This principle is repeated eight times in the QUR'AN in various *suras* (chapters).

[63] QUR'AN, sura aal Imran 3:145.

[64] QUR'AN, sura al-An'am 6:12.

[65] QUR'AN, sura Ghafir 40:17.

[66] Gerhard Bowering, *The Concept of Time in Islam*, 141 PROCEED. AMER. PHIL. SOC. 55, at 58 (March 1997). In Hindu mythology, Kali is the goddess of time and death.

[67] *See* Lind Zagzebski, *Eternity and Fatalism in* GOD, ETERNITY, AND TIME 65-80 (eds. Christian Tapp, Edmund Runggaldier)(Asshgate, 2011).

[68] QUR'AN, sura al-Jathiya 45:24.

[69] Id.

[70] QUR'AN, sura al-Jathiya 45:24.

[71] Tafsir Ibn Kathir on QUR'AN sura al-Jathiya 45:24 available at http://www.qtafsir.com/index.php?option=com_content&task=view&id=2050&Itemid=101

[72] QUR'AN, sura al-Jathiya 45:27. Heen may be a duration of mere seconds and minutes or of years and centuries.

[73] QUR'AN, sura al-Insan 76:1.

[74] Id. It uses distinct words to describe the various quantifications of time.

[75] QUR'AN, sura al-Jathiya 45:24.

[76] QUR'AN, sura al-Baqara 2:36.

[77] QUR'AN, sura al Ma'idah 5:101. This instruction was consistent with the broader theme that God desires convenience and not hardship for His creatures.

[78] Liaquat Ali Khan, Temporality of Law, McGoerge L. Rev.

[79] Qur'an Al-Baqara, 2:264. This parable is used to describe persons who give charity for display.

[80] Qur'an 9:70.

[81] Aristotle, PHYSICS (NuVision Pub. 2004).

[82] QUR'AN, sura al-Insan 76:1

[83] Liaquat Ali Khan, *Fana and Baqa Infinities of Islamic Law*, 7 U. ST. THOMAS L. REV. 511 (2010),

[84] Sun provides the concept of the year whereas the moon provides the concept of a month. Solar year and lunar month are central to the conception of time. Even solar calendars would have been confusing without the supportive notion of lunar month.

[85] QUR'AN, sura Ibrahim 14:33

[86] Id. (trans. Yusuf Ali).

[87] QUR'AN, sura Ibrahim 14:33.

[88] Id. (Trans. Asad).

[89] QUR'AN, sura al-Insan 76:1. Note #2. (Asad translation brings out the anthropocentric misconceptions of time),

[90] QUR'AN, sura Ibrahim 14:33 (trans. Pikhall)

[91] Ibn Kathir, Tafsir, Sura Ibrahim, Describing some of Allah's Tremendous favors, available online http://www.tafsir.com/default.asp?sid=14&tid=26580.

[92] Madudi, THE MEANING OF THE QUR'AN, *Sura Ibrahim*, description 44

[93] Id. It appears that Yusuf Ali's interpretation of *sakhkhar* (as subject to human beings) has little support in the juristic community. As discussed above, neither time and nor the vehicles of temporality are deities independent of God. They are subject to God's Law. Just as deities exercise no control over time, similarly human beings exercise no control over time. Time is God's creation and only God has sovereignty over time. However, human beings may benefit from practical uses of time and they may arrange and coordinate their personal and social affairs by counting and recording practical temporality.

[94] Several verses of the Qur'an mention the four vehicles of temporality--sun, moon, day, and night—to construct a practical system of time. One verse mentions these four vehicles together to lay the foundation for counting time. "God is the cleaver of the daybreak, and He has appointed the night for stillness, and the sun and the moon for measuring (time)."QUR'AN, sura al-An'am 6:96.

[95] QUR'AN, sura at-Tauba 9:36.

[96] It is important to note that Muslims do not worship the moon though the moon was an object of worship among Arabs before the rise of Islam.

[97] QUR'AN, sura al-Baqara 2: 189.

[98] For example, Jewish and Chinese lunar calendars add months to synchronize them with solar calendars.

[99] Some of the known calendars are Aztec, Maya, Hindu, Zoroastrian, Persian, Hebrew, Islamic, Ethiopian, Julian, and Gregorian. The Persian and the Gregorian calendars are identical to the extent that each calendar has 365 days and the leap year has 366 days. In the Persian calendar, however, 6 months are of 31 days, 5 months are of 30 days and the last month is of 29 days, except in the leap year when it also is of 30 days. The Gregorian calendar was derived from the Roman calendar, which was modified by Julius Caesar (46 B.C.), Augustus Caesar (8 B.C.), and Pope Gregory XIII(1582).

[100] Karima Diane Alavi, *Pillars of Religion and Faith* in 5 VOICES OF ISLAM 21 (ed. Vincent J. Cornell)(Greenwood, 2006)(explaining the impact of moon sighting in different regions of the world).

[101] Id.

[102] Saudi Arabia, for example, uses the astronomical calendar to determine Muslim holidays, such as eids.

[103] *See* Reuven Firestone, AN INTRODUCTION TO ISLAM for Jews 206-7 (Jewish Publication Society, 2006). Thus, 34 lunar years approximately equal to 33 solar years.

[104] For example, a meeting may be held on the third Wednesday of the month of Ramadhan. This notification/reminder is as informative as is the 19th of February.

[105] QUR'AN, sura Yunus 10:5. See also QUR'AN, sura al-Isra 17:12.

[106] QUR'AN, sura Ya-Sin 36:40.

[107] QUR'AN, sura Ya-Sin 36:40.

[108] QUR'AN, sura ar-Rahman 55:5. *See also*, sura al-Anbiya 21:33.

[109] (Ironically, Khayyam was known in his own time more as a man of mathematics rather than poetry, which laid dormant for two hundred years even in the Muslim world.) David W. Tschanz, Omar Khayyam—a Poet with a Flair of Numbers, Islam Online, available at <http://www.islamonline.net/english/science/2003/07/article04.shtml>

[110] David W. Tschanz, *Omar Khayyam—a Poet with a Flair of Numbers*, Islam Online, available at <http://www.islamonline.net/english/science/2003/07/article04.shtml>

[111] Khayyam was a member of the eight member team, which constructed the first most accurate calendar in the history of the world, and perhaps even more precise than the Gregorian calendar that the World now uses.

[112] W. Hope-Jones, *Calendar Reform* (in Correspondence), 45 The Mathematical Gazette 340-341 (December, 1961); Calendar Reform (in Correspondence), 46 MATH. GAZETTE 176 (May 1962).

[113] Hope-Jones, (1961) Id.

[114] David W. Tschanz, *Omar Khayyam—a Poet with a Flair of Numbers*, Islam Online, available at <http://www.islamonline.net/english/science/2003/07/article04.shtml>

[115] The Gregorian calendar was implemented in 1582. The Gregorian calendar was adopted in England in 1752. This adoption eliminated 11 days because the Julian calendar had forwarded the time by three quarters of a day a century. The sudden elimination of 11 days caused riots, as the people's birthdays and other historical events were perforce readjusted.

[116] Ah, but my computations, people say
Reduced the year to a better reckoning?—Nay
Twas only striking from the calendar
Unborn tomorrow, and dead yesterday.

[117] Every August, Awa Odori festival is held in Tokushima City, Japan, to honor the Buddhist O-bon, the days when the spirits of the dead return to their ancestral homes. The spirits are welcomed with the "dance of the fools," i.e., dancing in a state of ecstasy and intoxication. Every July, Las Fiestas de San Fermin takes place in Pamplona, Northern Spain, in the honor of Saint Fermin. In addition to dancing and wood-chopping, the festival is known for running with the bulls in the narrow streets of the city. Every year before Lent (March), the Venice Carnival celebrates "intrigue, mystery, and concealed identity." The centuries old tradition of wearing masks and causing mischief amidst Venetian canals and meandering streets attract tourists from all over the world. Festivals such as Octoberfest, Mardi Gras, La Tomatina, and the Thanksgiving Day celebrate seasons, the sowing and reaping of crops, real and fantasized victories--all tied to the solar calendar.

[118] Hava Lazarus-Yafeh, *Muslim Festivals*, 25 NUMEN 52 (April 1978).

[119] QUR'AN, sura Yunus 10:5.

[120] QUR'AN, sura an-Naml 27:40.

[121] *See, for example*, CONVENTION ON THE RIGHTS OF THE CHILD, Art. 1 (defining child as a human being below the age of eighteen years).

[122] Except Saudi Arabia, most Muslim states fix the voting age at eighteen years. http://chartsbin.com/view/re6

[123] "It would be administratively unwieldy and economically wasteful if the law was to evaluate each person on a case by case basis to assess whether the person has developed the requisite moral and intellectual maturity to enter into contracts." *See* Liaquat Ali Khan, *Temporality of Law*, 40 MCGEORGE L. REV. 33 (2008.)

[124] For example, the President of Pakistan must not be less than forty-five years of age. PAK. CONST. Art. 41(2).

[125] The Fair Labor Standards Act generally prohibits the employment of minors in work declared hazardous by the Secretary of Labor (such as work involving excavation or operations involving power-driven equipment). *See* Thomas E. Perez, U.S. Department of Labor, Youth & Labor: Age Requirements, http://www.dol.gov/dol/topic/youthlabor/agerequirements.htm.

[126] Employers may consider age as a bona fide occupational qualification. See generally Martin Schiff, The Age Discrimination in Employment Act: Whither the Bona Fide Occupational Qualification and Law Enforcement Exemptions?, 67 ST. JOHN'S L. REV. 1 (1993).

[127] Liaquat Ali Khan, *Temporality of Law*, *supra* note at -.

[128] QUR'AN, sura an- Nisa 4:6.

[129] Id.

[130] QUR'AN sura al-Haj 22:5.

[131] There is controversy over when life begins. For many, life begins at conception. *See*, for example, American Convention on Human Rights, article 1.

[132] Under the Age Discrimination in Employment Act of 1967 (ADEA), it is "unlawful for an employer . . . to fail or refuse to hire or to discharge any individual or otherwise discriminate against any individual with respect to his compensation, terms, conditions, or privileges of employment, because of such individual's age." 29 U. S. C. § 623(a)(1).

[133] Dail A. Neugarten (ed.), THE MEANINGS OF AGE 37-38 (Univ. Chicago Press, 1996).

[134] QUR'AN, sura al-Kahf 18:46.

[135] For example, a judge of the Pakistan Supreme Court must retire at the age of sixty five years. PAK. CONST. Art. 179.

[136] In 1977, Former U.S. Senator William Brock challenged the constitutionality of mandatory retirement saying, "As far as I am concerned, if you are capable of holding a job, it does not matter how old you are, you ought to be able to hold it, I do not see how, under the Constitution, somebody can automatically say you cannot have a job because you happen to be 67 years old." *See* Cong. Special Committee on Aging. The Next Steps in Combating Age Discrimination in Employment: With Special Reference to Mandatory Retirement Policy. 95th Cong., 1st Sess. Washington (1977).

[137] For a comparative employment dismissal criteria, including the American at-will dismissals, *see* Samuel Estreicher & Jeffrey M. Hirsch, *Comparative Wrongful Dismissal Law: Reassessing American Exceptionalism,* 92 N.C. L. REV. 343 (2014).

[138] The debate over mandatory retirement has gathered momentum in many countries. A more flexible approach suggests that productivity rather than an arbitrary chronological cut-off age is a more rational criterion for retirement. *See* Ibiwoye et al. *Mandatory or Flexible: Whither Retirement Age Policy?* 3 KCA J. BUS. MANG. 57 (2011) available at http://www.ajol.info/index.php/kjbm/article/view/65450/53138

[139] QUR'AN sura al-Baqara 2:280.

[140] QUR'AN, sura an-Nisa 4:103.

[141] Narrated Ibn 'Umar: Allah's Apostle said: Islam is based on (the following) five (principles): 1. To testify that none has the right to be worshipped but Allah and Muhammad is Allah's Apostle. 2. To offer the (compulsory congregational) prayers dutifully and perfectly. 3. To pay Zakat (i.e. obligatory charity). 4. To perform Hajj. (i.e. Pilgrimage to Mecca) 5. To observe fast during the month of Ramadan. SAHIH BUKHARI, Bk # 2, Hadith #7.

[142] Jabir b. 'Abdullah reported that the Messenger of Allah said: The similitude of five prayers is like an overflowing river passing by the gate of one of you in which he washes five times daily Hasan said: No filthiness can remain on him. SAHIH MUSLIM, Bk #4, Hadith #1411.

[143] Narrated Abdullah ibn Abbas: The Apostle of Allah (peace_be_upon_him) recited the supplication (Qunut) daily for a month at the noon, afternoon, sunset, night and morning prayers. When he said: "Allah listens to him who praises Him" in the last rak'ah, invoking a curse on some clans of Banu Sulaym, Ri'l, Dhakwan and Usayyah, and those who were standing behind him said: Amen. Sunan Abu Dawud, Bk #8, Hadith #1438.

[144] SAHIH BUKHARI, Bk. # 10, Hadith # 535 & 540.

[145] Narrated Abu Huraira: The Prophet said, "The prayer offered in congregation is twenty five times more superior (in reward) to the prayer offered alone in one's house or in a business center. . ." SAHIH BUKHARI Bk. # 8, Hadith # 466.

[146] A'isha reported: Fatimah b. Abu Hubaish came to the Apostle and said: I am a woman whose blood keeps flowing (even after the menstruation period). I am never purified; should I, therefore, abandon prayer? He (the Holy Prophet) said: Not at all, for that is only a vein, and is not a menstruation, so when menstruation comes, abandon prayer, and when it ends wash the blood from yourself and then pray. SAHIH MUSLIM, Bk #3, Hadith #652.

[147] Narrated Ibn Abbas : The Prophet once stayed for nineteen days and prayed shortened prayers. So when we travel led (and stayed) for nineteen days, we used to shorten the prayer but if we travelled (and stayed) for a longer period we used to offer the full prayer. SAHIH BUKHARI, Bk #20, Hadith #186.

[148] QUR'AN, sura al-Baqara 2:155

[149] Id. 2:185.

[150] *Iddat* is also required in the case of divorce. Consistent with Islam's inherent flexibility with respect to rules, however, if a marriage is not consummated and divorce occurs, no *iddat* is required. QUR'AN, sura Ahzab 33:49. This is so because a marriage without consummation is unlikely to build a strong spousal relationship.

[151] QUR'AN, sura al-Baqara 2:234.

[152] QUR'AN, sura al-Baqara 2:234 (Yusuf Ali). The *iddat* is also prescribed in cases of divorce. Note that the waiting period for a menstruating woman is different from one for women on menopause. *See* sura al-Baqara 2:228. In divorces, the *iddat* for menstruating women is measured in menstrual periods and not in lunar or solar months. Id.

[153] Id.

[154] For a more detailed coverage of this topic, *see* THE ISLAMIC LAW OF PERSONAL STATUS (Jamal J. Nasar, edit., 1990)

[155] QUR'AN, sura al-Baqara 2:240. This maintenance is waived if the widow voluntarily leaves the husband's house. Id.

[156] QUR'AN, sura al-Baqara 2:240.

[157] Jamal, *supra* note --- at 154.

[158] For a Western commentary on Islamic slavery, *see* W.G. Clarence-Smith, ISLAM AND THE ABOLITION OF SLAVERY 22 (Oxford Univ. Press, 2006).

[159] Even the 1926 Slavery Convention, amended in 1953, takes a flexible, though firm, commitment, to abolish slavery. Under Article 2, the parties undertake "(t)o bring about, progressively and as soon as possible, the complete abolition of slavery in all its forms." Id. Most Muslim states independent in 1926, including Afghanistan, Egypt, Iraq, Syria, and Turkey, ratified the Convention.

[160] *See* David Waines, AN INTRODUCTION TO ISLAM 97-99 (Cambridge Univ. Press, 2003)(stating that slavery is more a part of family law rather than property law as most slaves are employed for household work.)

[161] QUR'AN, sura al-Baqara 2: 221.

[162] Id.

[163] SAHIH BUKHARI, Book #46, Hadith #693.

[164] SAHIH BUKHARI, Book #44, Hadith #681.

[165] QUR'AN, sura an- Nisa 4: 92. The rule is a bit more complex than stated here. Compensation is exempted if the deceased belongs to a people at war. However, freeing a slave is a common obligation regardless of whether the deceased belongs to a people at war or to a people at peace or to a people with whom there is a treaty of alliance.

[166] Id.

[167] QUR'AN, sura al- Mujadilah 58:3. Abu Ala Maududi explains: "Among the Arabs it often so happened that during a family quarrel, the husband in the heat of the moment would say to his wife: *Ant-i alayya ka-zahr-i ammi* which literally means: "You are for me as the back of my mother." But its real meaning is: "To have sexual relations with you would be like having sexual relations with my mother." Such words are still uttered by the foolish people, who, as the result of a family quarrel, declare the wife to be like their mother, or sister, or daughter, and make her unlawful for themselves like the prohibited women. This is called *zihar*." Abu Ala Maududi, THE MEANING OF QURAN, sura al-Mujadilah 58:3, note 3. The Qur'an condemned the practice of *zihar* in strong words, calling it a lie. Id. 58: 1-4.

[168] Id. 58:4.

[169] SAHIH BUKHARI, Book #2, Hadith #29.

[170] John R. Bradley, BEHIND THE VEIL OF VICE 123-124(Macmillan, 2008).

[171] "Narrated Aisha, Ummul Mu'minin: Ghudayf ibn al-Harith reported: I asked Aisha: Have you seen the Apostle of Allah washing (because of defilement) at the beginning of the night or at the end? She replied: Sometimes he would take a bath at the beginning of the night and sometimes at the end. Thereupon I exclaimed: Allah is most Great. All Praise be to Allah Who made this matter accommodative. I again asked her: What do you think, did the Apostle of Allah say the *witr* prayer (additional prayer after obligatory prayer at night) in the beginning of the night or at the end? She replied: Sometimes he would say the *witr* prayer at the beginning of the night and sometimes at the end. I exclaimed: Allah is most Great. All praise be to Allah Who made the matter

accommodative. Again I asked her: What do you think, did the Apostle of Allah recite the QUR'AN (in the prayer) loudly or softly? She replied: Sometimes he would recite loudly and sometimes softly. I exclaimed: Allah is most Great. All praise be to Allah Who made the matter flexible." SUNAN ABUDAWUD Bk #1, Hadith # 0226.

[172] QUR'AN, sura al-Baqara 2:286.

[173] QUR'AN, sura al-Araf 7:199

[174] *See* Asad translation of 7:199 and the accompanying note # 162.

[175] Narrated 'Abdullah bin AzZubair: (The Verse) "Hold to forgiveness; command what is right..." was revealed by Allah except in connection with the character of the people. 'Abdullah bin Az-Zubair said: Allah ordered His Prophet to forgive the people their misbehavior (towards him). SAHIH BUKHARI, Bk. # 60, Hadith # 167.

[176] About 650 million people, approximating 10% of the world's population, live with a disability. Disability rates are higher in developing countries, among the poor, among groups with lower educational attainment, and among women. Women and girls with disabilities are beaten, raped, and forcible sterilized. Mortality among children with disabilities is as high as 80 percent. Warfare has been a cause of producing persons with disabilities. For these and other facts, *see Some Facts about Persons with Disabilities* http://www.un.org/disabilities/convention/facts.shtml

[177] QUR'AN, sura Abasa 80: 1-10

[178] QUR'AN, sura Abasa 80: 1-10

[179] The information about the Convention and its text is available at http://www.un.org/disabilities/convention/conventionfull.shtml

[180] The following Muslim states have ratified this Convention. Afghanistan, Algeria, Azerbaijan, Bahrain, Bangladesh, Bosnia and Herzegovina, Brunei, Burkina Faso, Chad, Egypt, Indonesia, Iran, Iraq, Jordan, Kazakhstan, Kyrgyzstan, Libya, Malaysia, Mauritania, Niger, Oman, Pakistan, Qatar, Saudi Arabia, Syria, Turkey, Uzbekistan, Yemen. Other countries with Muslims as the largest group, such as Nigeria, have also ratifies the treaty.

[181] Convention on the Rights of Persons with Disabilities, Arts. 3, 8.

[182] Hidayet Ayder, Dreaming in the Life of Prophet Muhammad *in* DREAMING IN CHRISTIANITY AND ISLAM 81 (ed. Kelly Bulkeley and others)(Rutgers University Press, 2009)(stating that dreams have favorable place in Islamic cognition).

[183] SAHIH BUKHARI, Bk. # 87, Hadith # 144.

[184] SAHIH MUSLIM, Bk.#029, Hadith #5621.

[185] Narrated Ibn 'Umar: Allah's Apostle said, "While I was sleeping, I saw that a cup full of milk was brought to me and I drank my fill till I noticed (the milk) its wetness coming out of my nails. Then I gave the remaining milk to 'Umar Ibn

Al-Khattab" The companions of the Prophet asked, "What have you interpreted (about this dream)? "O Allah's Apostle ,!" he replied, "(It is religious) knowledge." SAHIH BUKHARI, Book #3, Hadith #82.

[186] SAHIH BUKHARI, Bk. # 87, Hadith # 144.

[187] "The commencement of the Divine Inspiration to Allah's Apostle was in the form of good dreams which came true like bright day light, and then the love of seclusion was bestowed upon him." SAHIH BUKHARI, Bk.# 1, Hadith #3.

[188] QUR'AN, sura al-Fath, 48:27.

[189]arrated 'Aisha: That the Prophet said to her, "You have been shown to me twice in my dream. I saw you pictured on a piece of silk and some-one said (to me). 'This is your wife.' When I uncovered the picture, I saw that it was yours. I said, 'If this is from Allah, it will be done." (Book #58, Hadith #235) SAHIH BUKHARI, Bk. # 62, Hadith # 15.

[190] QUR'AN sura as-Saffat 37:102.

[191] QUR'AN, sura Yusuf, 12:43.

[192] Quran, sura Yusuf 12:36.

[193] QUR'AN, sura al-Anbiya, 21:5.

[194] Alan J. Friedman & Carol C. Donley, EINSTEIN AS MYTH AND MUSE 85-88 (CUP Archive, 1989).

[195] Nivoldo Tro, CHEMISTRY IN FOCUS 149 (Cengage Learning, 2012).

[196] Jocelyn Sharlet, PATRONAGE AND POETRY IN THE ISLAMIC WORLD 8 (I.B. Taurus, 2011)(stating how Muslim poets regarded poetry as the basis for making sense of ethical and social status). Narrated Ubai bin Ka'b: Allah's Apostle said, "Some poetry contains wisdom." SAHIH BUKHARI, Book #73, Hadith #166. This hadith has been a strong incentive for Muslims to develop the art of poetry.

[197] Jacques Sesiano, AN INTRODUCTION TO THE HISTORY OF ALGEBRA 93 (American Mathematical Soc., 2009)(narrating the introduction of Muslim-invented algebra to Europe after the re-conquest of Spain in the fifteenth century).

[198] QUR'AN, sura ar-Rum 30:8; 30:21. In these verses, the QUR'AN invites human beings to reflect upon the creation and love that God has implanted in the hearts of men and women who are attracted to each other.

[199] Bryn Barnard, THE GENIUS OF ISLAM 9 (Random House, 2013).

[200] Titus Burckhardt, ART OF ISLAM 11 (World Wisdom, 2009).

[201] Elizabeth pepper & John Wilcock, MAGICAL AND MYSTICAL SITES 132 (Red Wheel/Weiser, 2000). Washington Irving (19783-1859), an American writer, wrote Tales of the Alhambra, a collection of essays and stories, a book instrumental in introducing the Alhambra to Americans.

[202] Lesley A. DuTemple, THE TAJ MAHAL (Twenty-First Century Books, 2003).

[203] QUR'AN, sura al-Anbiya 21:107.

[204] The Prophet Muhammad's Last Sermon, available at https://www.islamicity.com/mosque/lastserm.htm

[205] QUR'AN, sura an-Nas 114:1-3.

[206] Basics of Becoming a Muslim, available at
https://www.islamicity.com/mosque/Muslim.htm

[207] Liaquat Ali Khan, *The Immutability of Divine Texts*, 2008 B.Y.U. L. Rev. 807 (2008).

[208] Inter-temporality may be distinguished from flexible interpretations. Flexible interpretations mean that a text may be interpreted in more than one way. Inter-temporality flexibility is inter-generational and may vary from one period to another.

[209] QUR'AN, sura al-Isra 17:77; sura al-Ahzab 33:62; sura Fatir 35:43.

[210] QUR'AN, sura an-Nisa 4:163.

[211] QUR'AN, sura al-Isra 17:55.

[212] QUR'AN, sura az-Zukhruf 43:4.

[213] Liaquat Ali Khan, *The Immutability of Divine Texts*, 2008 B.Y.U. L. Rev. 807 (2008).

[214] God's immutability has been copiously, though fruitlessly, explored in German philosophical and theological literature. Schelling, Hegel, & Isaac Dorner have refined the concept of God's immutability. *See* Robert F. Brown, *Schelling and Dorner on Divine Immutability*, 53 J. AM. ACAD. RELIGION 237 (Jun. 1985)( Islam prohibits speculation about God).

[215] QUR'AN, sura Alaq, 96:5.

[216] Instincts and knowledge, however, may lead or mislead individuals and nations. Instincts and knowledge may serve as facilitators or barriers in comprehending Divine Law. When instincts and knowledge are harnessed, their combined force may facilitate the understanding of Divine Law. When instincts disregard knowledge or knowledge ignores instincts, the separation may interfere with the reception of Divine Law. When both instincts and knowledge go astray, the error is compounded and the nation rejects Divine Law. The nation drifts away from Divine Law.

[217] QUR'AN sura al-Anbiya 21:33.

[218] For the relationship between Islam and science over the past centuries, *see generally* Muzaffar Iqbal, SCIENCE AND ISLAM (Greenwood, 2007).

[219] Antonin Scalia, Originalism: *The Lesser Evil*, 57 U. CIN. L. REV. 849, 863 (1989).

[220] Id.

[221] Id.

[222] QUR'AN, sura al-Baqara 2:272.

[223] QUR'AN, sura al Nahl 16:93 (trans; Muhsin Khan).

[224] L. Ali Khan & Hisham Ramadan, CONTEMPORARY IJTIHAD (Edinburgh Univ. Press, 2012).

[225] Id. at

[226] Ali Khan, The Opening of the Basic Code: The Second Era of Ijtihad, 1 UNIV. ST. THOMAS L. J. 341 (2003).

[227] There are 57 states on the world that identify themselves to be Muslim states. All are part of the Organization of Islamic Cooperation, and inter-governmental organization. The 57 states are listed at http://www.oic-oci.org/oicv2/states/

[228] Malaysia is a religiously pluralistic society with Muslims constituting 61% of the population. About 20% practice Buddhism. About 15% practice Christianity and Hinduism. The United Arab Emirates is a Muslim Arab state with the majority of population is immigrants from South Asia.

[229] See generally Todd Knoop, GLOBAL FINANCING IN EMERGING MARKET ECONOMIES (Routledge, 2013)(Malaysia is a leading Muslim state in Islamic banking, Islamic bonds, called sukuks, and Islamic international banking).

[230] Selim Cakir & Faezeh Raei, SUKUK VS. EUROBONDS 3(International Monetary Fund, 2007)(Malaysia and the Gulf region are the main hubs for the issuance of sukuk).

[231] It is narrated on the authority of 'Abdullah son of 'Umar that the Messenger of Allah said: (The superstructure of) al-Islam is raised on five (pillars), testifying (the fact) that there is no god but Allah, that Muhammad is His bondsman and messenger, and the establishment of prayer, payment of Zakat, Pilgrimage to the House (Ka'ba) and the fast of Ramadan. SAHIH MUSLIM, Bk #1, Hadith #20.

www.ingramcontent.com/pod-product-compliance
Lightning Source LLC
Chambersburg PA
CBHW020553220526
45463CB00006B/2287